Keep Walking,
Your Heart Will Catch Up

a Camino de Santiago journey

Bob,
Thank you for
being part of the
book's early readers.
I appreciate your comments.
Buen Camino —
Cathay

Cathay O. Reta

ISBN 978-1-09834-050-6

www.cathayreta.com

To David

We always wanted to return to Spain,
I just never thought I'd be doing it without you.
You're forever in my heart.

Table of Contents

Acknowledgements

I am grateful for many people who helped to get this book into print.

First and foremost, thank you to AnaMaria Ruiz who has encouraged and supported me from the beginning – from the idea to do the hike, through the year of training and planning, and most significantly in doing the work to actually write and publish. I appreciate her support as friend, agent, business manager, critic and cheerleader.

My friends Peter Casas and David Ramos walked the Camino in 2016. Peter is the first who told me about the Camino. I thank Peter and David for leading the way.

I am forever grateful to my friend Kathleen Horstmeyer, who virtually walked with me. I texted her regularly from the Camino as a safety precaution. At least someone would know where I was last seen if anything happened to me and I didn't return home. I appreciate her encouragement and her tolerance of my daily complaints.

I appreciate the early readers of my first drafts. Their feedback and suggestions helped to bring the book to publication. They gave me courage to share my story. Thank you, Pamela Cibbarelli, Wendy Okuda, Donna Vallesio-Valkos, Joe Verdugo, Susan Walters, and Bob Weaver. Also, a big thank you to Claudia Sandoval for help with book cover layout.

I am thankful to Ray Corder for many things, but especially for his belief in me. I am thankful for his push for me to "get in there and finish the book" when I was procrastinating so badly.

Lastly, I'm thankful for Hannah Hurnard. What serendipity it was to have selected her book *Hinds' Feet on High Places* to take with me on my journey. It was written in 1955. I read it in the '70s. Then I lived it myself on this pilgrimage. I had no idea this book would take on such a prominent role in my pilgrimage.

Preface

They say the Camino de Santiago is magical, mystical. I think the magic of the Camino de Santiago is the way she draws you into life's possibilities. She's the jokester who taps you on the shoulder then jumps to the other side, leaving you bewildered. If your heart is open and you listen closely, you might hear her whisper. Your eyes might open wide, maybe your lashes will grow moist. Appreciation for life might flourish. If you listen closely, you will begin to know yourself and to better understand what you bring to the world. That's what I think.

Some say that the Camino runs along a spiritual vortex, complete with magical powers. *The Camino provides you with what you need.* That has been affirmed by many, many stories told by pilgrims for a good many years. For example, one friend shared he and his small group arrived at a town where they had planned to spend the night, but there was no more room at the hostel. He stood in the middle of the street, bewildered and wondering what to do next when a car pulled up. The driver asked, "Do you need a place to stay?" She took them to other accommodations.

On the Camino I always carried one plastic water bottle with me to refill, then change it out for a new one every day or two. At one point I was thinking that I need to trade out my plastic water bottle for a fresh one. Three minutes later I turned a corner and there was a stand set up in a shade. Its owner called out, "You need a fresh bottle of water."

I think it, and it appears. That type of experience happened a few times. Coincidence? I like to think not. I like to think that's the charm and the romance of the Camino.

I felt drawn to hike the Camino de Santiago three years after my husband passed away. I was a 64-year-old widow, seeking what to do with my next 30 years. I learned to embrace the Camino like a trusted friend. We had quite an affair over our 37 days together. Days I will never forget, days I will always treasure.

Maybe one day you'll have opportunity to walk the Camino de Santiago yourself. Or perhaps you'll be caressed by her charm as you find yourself mirrored in my experience. I hope so. I hope that as you read my pilgrimage, you will experience an internal awakening of your own.

I hope that in these pages the Camino will tap you on the shoulder, bewilder you and unravel your secrets. I hope that she will give you hope and put a smile on your face. I hope that you will find hardship is not necessarily a bad thing. Sometimes it is the most direct path to discovering the beauty and truth of your being.

Buen camino!

CHAPTER 1

Saying Goodbye

July 31, 2016, 2:30 a.m.

"Look at me," said the Lord to me.

I turned my attention to Him, my hands still clasped around David's cold fist. His eyes were closed, he was mostly asleep, barely responsive.

"Look at me," the Lord repeated. "I've got it from here."

I stepped back understanding that these next hours were between David and his Lord – the God who kept him sheltered in His love.

Four years earlier my 33-year marriage had taken a drastic left turn. In October 2012 David had a stroke which affected his left side. That was followed by a heart attack in November and a stroke on the right side in December. We had been on quite a roller coaster ride since then. There were severe drops that knocked the breath out of us both, and then euphoric highs when we would see progress and signs that he was getting better. . . but always ending in another deep dip down. In his last year he was mostly in slow decline with a number of small strokes and other complications.

A few days earlier David had suddenly lost most of his vision. While watching TV he could no longer distinguish anyone, the screen was just a blob. He could see some from the peripheral on each side, but not straight ahead. I held up two fingers in front of him; he could only see one. He was not willing to go to the hospital.

It is perhaps inconceivable that someone with his health history, facing such a serious event, would not go to the hospital – and inconceivable that I would agree to that. On the other hand, after four years of running in and out of emergency rooms, there had come a point to which we no longer responded the same as someone else. We knew there was not much that the medical profession could do. Looking back, it is obvious that the decisions not to continue were happening from this point, maybe earlier.

The next morning David's normal vision returned. For the following few days he felt *out of it*. He was mostly sleeping; barely responsive. He would not eat. On the third day I insisted that we go to the hospital. He agreed.

It was a familiar routine. As with every time he went to the emergency room with signs of stroke, they ran a cat scan. But this time, for the first time, the scan showed blood on the brain. A lot of it. He had a serious brain hemorrhage. They transferred him to the hospital in Fontana where a neurosurgeon was on duty and waiting to operate, if needed.

Continuing at his side, I emotionally stepped out of the way to leave David with God for their discussion. I laid down on the bed set up for me in his hospital room, and I fell asleep.

Awaking, I remembered that a few weeks ago I kept hearing a whisper, *Your husband is dying.*

Gasp. "Who is this? God, is that you? No, it must be the devil. I won't have any of that!" I closed my ears to those words but they continued in light refrain. David had become weaker and I stayed home from work to be with him, suspecting that the phrase was a call to set priorities. It was for me to put David first and never have to regret that I chose work over him.

One afternoon I curled up on the couch within a hand's reach of him. I told him I was keeping an eye on him. I suggested he keep an eye on me, too. I rested and slept, like a loyal dog at her master's feet. I needed him to know I was there for him. And for my sake, I needed to be there at his feet.

Now as I heard the Lord tell me that He would take it from here, I was sure it was his voice. I also knew He was telling me that indeed it had been him whispering to me.

"Yes, Lord. I do know your voice." I had become confused and unsure in previous days. It was inconceivable that God, the giver of life, would tell me my husband is dying. Now I understood. I remembered a night in Guadalajara, Mexico in the early 1980s. I woke up in the middle of the night with awareness that my father had died. I cried. I waited for a phone call which never came. I cried out to God that I wasn't ready to lose my father. We didn't have a good relationship. He told me to work on the relationship, and I did. When my father passed away a dozen years later, our relationship was solid. I have forever been thankful for the Spirit shaking me up, jostling me awake that night to make a point.

With reassurance, without fear or panic, I now understood this was the Lord's grace to me once again. The Lord was preparing me. His whisper was an awakening, calling me to live like today is all I have. It is all that I have. It is all that any of us have.

David left the hospital after a few days. Soon afterwards, in one of the rare moments when he was able to speak clearly, he told me how tired he was. He said to me, "Cathay, let me go."

I wanted to make sure I wasn't reading anything into it. "Go where, David? Are you talking about going to be with the Lord?"

"Yes, let me go," he said.

"Ok, I understand," I told him. "I love you. I'll miss you, but you can go." David passed away twelve days later.

David and Cathay Reta, 2015, married 33 years

The Camino

Two years after David passed away I found myself being pulled to hike the Camino de Santiago – the Way of St. James – a 483-mile trail across northern Spain. I first heard of it in the final months of David's life. Our good friends Peter Casas and David Ramos were going to hike it. I wished I could go as well. I loved the idea of such a great adventure, but it was impossible for me.

Still, the thought lingered. The thought never left the back of my mind.

David passed just before Peter and David left for Spain. In his honor, they each carried a stone from David's fish aquarium to leave at the *Cruz de Ferro* (Iron Cross), a landmark along the trail. It is customary for hikers to take a stone from home to add to the pile at the foot of the cross. Every stone is significant to someone. Every stone carries someone's memories, released burdens, hopes realized. When I gave Peter the stones I had no idea that I would also one day lay a stone at that cross.

The Way of St. James, the *Camino*, has been travelled by pilgrims for hundreds of years to reach the cathedral in Santiago de Compostela. It is one of three main Christian pilgrimage sites, along with Rome and Jerusalem. In its zenith, the 11th – 12th centuries, it is reported that as many as 1,000 pilgrims a day visited the cathedral in Santiago where the remains of St. James, the disciple of Jesus, is said to be interred. St. Frances of Assisi was one such pilgrim in 1214.

There are several paths – or *caminos* – that lead to Santiago. They include the Portuguese which originates in Lisbon, Portugal, the Spanish which travels from southern Spain northward, the northern route which hugs the coast of northern Spain, and French routes which begin as far away as Paris before reaching the Pyrenees. The most popular route – the French Way – was featured in the 2010 film *The Way* with Martin Sheen and Emilio Estevez. The French Way now records over 200,000 visitors on its roads every year. Being so well traveled, it is one of the best-marked paths and has plenty of hostels to stay at along the way. The French Way starts in St. Jean Pied de Port, France at the foot of the Pyrenees, crosses into Spain and runs westward across the country to Santiago de Compostela.

There is evidence that this was a well-travelled route long before it became a Christian symbol. Some say that its path follows the stars of the Milky Way to Finesterre, to the coastal cliffs which in ancient times were believed to be the end of the earth. Many pilgrims take an extra three or four days to walk on past Santiago to Finesterre still today. Some people say that ley lines create a spiritual vortex across the Camino path, making it a healing journey, joining body and spirit. Others say there is no support for such theory. Still, many – if not most – who have travelled the Camino do attribute some kind of mystical power to what they experienced along the way. I don't know anything about that, but I did find myself being *called*. I knew it was something I had to do.

A Rite of Passage

I had not hiked in years. I had even forgotten how much I used to enjoy a good hike in my younger days, in my 20s. The most memorable was hiking to Indian Gardens, halfway down the Grand Canyon with my friends, Sue Collins and Mary Gibeau. Somewhere along the way hiking had simply fallen away as an activity for me and I had taken on a sedentary life. Now I was planning the walk of a lifetime – almost 500 miles.

On my 64th birthday I decided that I would like to do something special to commemorate my 65th year. That's when I set in my heart to walk the Camino. I decided that I would celebrate my 65th birthday in Spain on the Camino de Santiago.

I was embarrassed to tell anyone of my plan. Me? Really? I would mention it as *I would like to* . . . Later it became, *I might.* Eventually it grew to a calculated declaration. *There's a 60% chance I'll hike the Camino,* . . . then it was 75%, then 80%. Even three months before going, up until I bought my plane ticket, I was calling it a 90-95% chance I would do the hike. It just seemed so incredulous to me that I could actually pull this off.

Me. Alone. At my age.

For a year I walked and hiked and prepared for the physical challenge. I broke in hiking boots and hiking sandals (I took both), practiced walking with a backpack, bought quick-dry clothes. I studied Camino forums and YouTube videos to learn what to take and what to not take.

I did a lot of reading. I learned that approximately 300,000 individuals made the journey in 2017. In one book, I landed on a chapter about making the hike a *rite of passage*. That sparked something within me. I knew this was my journey. I stopped reading for a moment to let the thought sink in.

I was drawn into a deep, dark forest that dissolved into blackness. An empty dark abyss. I cried. I felt sorrow, and I slowly came to understand that I had not just lost my husband. I had lost half of me. I was half dark and void. Trying to fill that space with otherness had only created more volume of darkness. The void could not be filled. It could not be covered over, nor chased away. That void could only be mourned.

I knew that when it was finished being mourned – at a time I was not privy to know – I would come out knowing myself once again.

For me, the Camino would be a pilgrimage. It would embody a rite of passage – a passage to becoming widowed. A widow, living in a different circumstance, a different time.

I sat in stillness. In darkness. Then I recorded my reaction in my journal:

Ah-ha! I'm in it now. I am actually in mourning. I let go and let the emotions carve their way through the tears and the angst. I feel pain and I don't want to stop feeling the pain. I want to be aware of every bit of it. It is somehow so very necessary. Right now, that is life to me. To mourn is to live in this moment. To

13

mourn is to acknowledge the void and give it space to be.

What is significant to me is that with tonight's revelation, with this drama, I have officially begun my pilgrimage. My rite of passage. My Camino starts now. Even as I prepare for the physical challenge it presents, I am also preparing inwardly. I am beginning to mourn what is gone. My life cannot be the same as it once was. What it will become is yet to be seen.

What is also clear and significant to me, is that mourning does not have to be equated with sadness. I can pass through this ritual in joy and gladness. And that is my intent.

Cathay at home, packed and ready to go.

The Journey Begins
July 4, 2019: Post Falls, Idaho to Paris, France

I fly to Paris to spend three days before taking the train to St. Jean Pied de Port (St. John *Foot of the Path*) on the French side of the Pyrenees to begin my Camino. I wander through Paris and reminisce the trip I had made in 1997 with David and our good friend Elvia. This time, however, I'm alone. It's a struggle. I find that I'm not liking Paris like I did back then.

I visit the familiar places, such as the Eiffel Tower, Musée d'Orsay, and the Louvre. I even find the hotel we stayed at on *Rue Cler*. It's the only hotel left now on this beautiful pedestrian street lined with sidewalk cafes. The fruit and vegetable stand next door to the hotel is still there. That's where we first tasted lychee fruit.

I find some new places we had somehow missed in my previous trip – the Trocadero, a walk along the Seine, and new patio cafes. I have some enjoyable moments, some relaxing and reflection. But for the most part I feel so alone. I can't find my place. I don't fit in.

My heels are in such pain. I had abused them in walking too much, too fast, too far throughout the previous year as I prepared for the hike. The result was Achilles Tendonitis – on both feet. Friends had encouraged me to postpone my trip for a year to let my heels recover, but I didn't. I knew I needed to do this now, this year. In Paris I planned on resting my heels by taking taxis rather than walking, but I don't. Somehow I just start walking, planning to go a short distance, but I keep extending that distance further and further. I don't know why I do this to myself, but I do.

In addition, I miss David. I resent being in the *City of Light* alone in darkness. My body hurts, the summer heat is overwhelming, my AirBnB is a dump, and I'm beginning to dread what lays ahead.

My journal entries describe this time in Paris:

July 5: Maybe this start is the first step. Maybe it's to break me down. Tear me down to nothing so I can build from there. It's puncturing numbness that surrounds me and keeps me from feeling anything. Puncturing my veneer so that the impurities – the lies, the stories I've told myself, the lack I've settled for – can all seep through and away from me.

Maybe. Maybe that's it. Or maybe it's just a shitty day.

July 6: I find myself slowing down, emptying my mind of the constant thoughts, constant chatter. Perhaps this is the preparation for Camino. Perhaps it is to experience calm, to be content in the now.

I fear to let my mind really rest. I fear I will find just how much I do miss David and just how much I feel lost and alone. Perpetual motion has kept me from going there. But go there, I must. Go there, I will.

July 7: Paris is good. It was just me out of sorts the first days – alone and scared. I'm still alone, but not so scared now. I think I know what I have to do. I have to be okay with aloneness, to accept and embrace solitude.

This is a re-set. I am emptying out all I thought I knew. Starting at a new place.

I am still scared, but so be it.

CHAPTER 2

"Owning our story can be hard but not nearly as difficult as spending our lives running from it."

- Brené Brown, The Gifts of Imperfection

July 8. Getting to St. Jean Pied de Port

The Camino has many lessons to share. At least that's what I've heard, and I look forward to learning. That's my mindset anyway. I quickly find out that what you learn may have a lot to do with how observant you are. My train from Paris to Bayonne, then to St. Jean Pied de Port was scheduled to arrive at 8:00 pm. However, through a series of delays, it is arriving closer to

11:30 pm. I'm not too happy about arriving in an unknown town so late, but there's nothing I can do about it.

As the train nears the station I notice a couple of young men stand and put rain covers over their backpacks and waterproof jackets over their well-framed, healthy, toned bodies. I wonder if I should pull out my rain poncho and my backpack's rain cover as well. Investigating the question, I look at the weather forecast on my iPhone. Rain is not expected for another three to four hours. I look at the large group in the back of the train. They aren't moving. They are just chatting and revving up in excitement and anticipation of the Camino. I sit still. I figure I'll go with the majority. If it is raining, I'll get out my rain gear in the station before heading down the street.

We arrive. The train doors open, and out I step onto the sidewalk in pouring rain. There is no building. We just empty out onto the street. How I wish I had taken a cue from the two young men who exited the train prepared rather than follow the herd kicking back, making no plans! I don't know where to go, or how to get to my hostel. I had planned to arrive in daylight with enough time to easily find the place. Thank God I had made a reservation at the hostel Makila before leaving Paris. Once I knew we'd be delayed, I had called ahead to let them know. Most hostels close and lock the doors at 10:00 pm, but the host said he would wait for me.

I take off up the street to try to catch a group walking together. I hope they will know the way to the main street. More specifically, I hope they can help me find my hostel. I struggle to put on my rain poncho while walking fast, and I run into a car—a *parked car*, thankfully. Then I realize that I put my poncho on backwards, so I can't pull the hood up over my head to keep dry. I'm getting more and more wet. I laugh at myself at how unprepared I am. It's kind of a nervous laugh, really.

This is not a good start. The only people in sight in this dark, wet town are quickly getting further away from me. I'm scared. Despite the burning pain in my heels, I run to catch up.

Fortunately, three of them stop under an awning. A young couple is trying to help a third man figure out where to find lodging since it's late and most hostels are closed now. I reach them and they direct me to my hostel, my *albergue* (the Spanish word for hostel). Turns out that they had stayed there before. They knew exactly where to send me—straight up, up, up the cobblestone street around the corner. I thank them for their help and the young man tells me, "That's what we do. We help each other on the Camino." That's reassuring since I obviously need help tonight and probably will again.

Off I go, as fast as I can while trying to not slip on the wet cobblestones. I ignore the pain in my heels and give up on any idea of not getting too wet. It's a steep climb. I'm winded.

The host, anxiously waiting for me while standing in the Makila doorway, is a welcome sight. Another traveler— or rather *pilgrim* as we are called on the Camino—is also waiting. She's sitting on the bench inside. Like me, she's wet and cold. The host had waited for me to get there before showing us both to our beds. He opens the door to a small room with four sets of bunk beds against the walls, with a narrow aisle in between. He points to the first two beds, telling us to be quiet since others are already asleep.

Quietly, using the flashlight from my phone, I change into a dry t-shirt, spread out the sleeping bag liner from my pack, and climb into bed. It has a curtain to draw for privacy, making a small cubicle. The other late arriver climbs into her cubicle across from mine.

I make mental note of my first lesson—learn from the experts. When you see people who obviously know more about what's going on than you, follow their lead. If I had done so, I could have at least arrived dry instead of all wet. When I watched the two young men inside the train car prepare for rain, an inner stirring was poking at me to do the same. Instead, I did nothing. I followed the majority out into the pouring rain, unprepared. *C'est la vie. That's life.* "But does it have to be?" I think. Maybe I can learn to do better.

On a warmer note, I think about how kind the young man and his girlfriend were to direct me to my room. They had actually walked to the street with me to make sure I didn't miss it. "On the Camino we help each other out," he had said. What a wonderful way to live. I wish people would be like that everywhere, all the time.

Day 1: July 9
St. Jean de Pied de Port – Roncesvalles (via bus)

At Camino hostels, or *albergues* as they are called in Spanish, pilgrims are usually required to leave by 8:00 am so that the host can clean and prepare the facility for the next group's arrival. I wake up early and go upstairs to the small dining room to grab something to eat before 8:00. Coffee, bread with butter and jam, and orange juice—the first of many traditional Camino breakfasts I will enjoy along the way.

The coffee is good, the bread satisfying, but the best part is the view. Most of the night's pilgrims have already left, so I sit at a wooden table by myself, looking out the open window over a most beautiful green and lush garden. The rain has left plant leaves glistening in the narrow courtyard. Small white houses in the distance are strikingly beautiful set against a green mountain. Pink flowers line the garden. I wish I knew the names of the vibrant blossoms. Sadly, I've never paid much attention to such details. I don't know the names of most flowers, plants or trees. As I look out the window this morning, I wish I had the vocabulary to describe them. I wish I were more in tune with nature's beauty, with her grace. I'm sorry I've never gotten to know Mother Earth and her offerings.

My roommate (and co-late arriver) comes in as I finish eating. I have a second cup of coffee to sit and visit with her. Amy is twenty-two years old and from South Korea. Her English is excellent. This is no surprise since she teaches English to elementary school children. At the same time, she is finishing her final year of study at the university and figuring out what to do with her life.

I learn that she had also begun her travel in Paris and injured her big toe while there. She shares that because of that injury she will have to take the bus this first day rather than walk the Napoleon Route over the Pyrenees to Roncesvalles.

That's my plan, too! With my Achilles injuries I would only damage my feet and jeopardize the whole trip to walk that first day. The Napoleon Route from St. Jean Pied de Port is a steep climb over the Pyrenees mountains – ascending 4757 feet over thirteen miles, and then it sharply descends 1296 feet for the final two and a half miles to Roncesvalles. Even if you break up the fifteen and a half miles into two days by staying overnight at the *albergue* in Orisson, it is still a difficult and potentially dangerous way to begin a long pilgrimage. Some people begin walking from the middle of France a day or two earlier so that their bodies can warm up by the time they tackle the Pyrenees. Some take the alternate Val Carlos Route which is not as steep but is still quite challenging. Others, like Amy and me, take the bus to Roncesvalles and begin the walk from there, from the Spanish side of the mountains. We decide to walk together.

Our first stop is the Pilgrim's Office, just two doors up from our *albergue*. I wish we had known that before walking to the bottom of the hill to look for it and finding out we have to re-trace our steps back up to where we started. At the office I get my official Pilgrim Passport, a map of thirty-four stages of the route which includes the kilometers and elevation of travel for each day, and a master list of contact information for many of the *albergues* along the trail.

St. Jean Pied de Port, a beautiful morning to start the journey.

The passport is the official document that pilgrims present to be able to stay at the hostels along the way. The hosts stamp the passport each day. At the end of the Camino I will present it to the Pilgrim's Office in Santiago de Compostela as proof that I did indeed earn the *Compostela* (the certificate of completion). I also pick up a scallop shell to attach to my backpack. It's a sign of the pilgrim on the Camino.

Our next stop is a small shop on the cobble stone street where we both buy trekking poles. After a lot of investigation about them before leaving the USA, I decided to buy mine here in France rather than try to carry them with me on the airplane. I didn't check luggage. I carried my backpack, filled with everything I would use over the next month and a half onto the plane. Unfortunately, most flights don't allow the poles as carry-on, so I'm happy to so easily find a sturdy, inexpensive set here.

The rain from the previous day left the beautiful, colorful city glistening in the fresh morning air, adding to our excitement.

To walk to Roncesvalles would have been glorious. I wish I could do that. I wish I had been wiser in preparing for the hike. Back home I kept walking each day, trying to work up to ten mile hikes, thinking my body would adjust and the foot pains would go away as I got used to it. I didn't realize that I had developed tendonitis, and the only way to take care of that is to rest. But the damage is done. Here I am. I will try to minimize further damage as I go. So I start out by bus.

Even traveling by bus is remarkable. Luminous green mountains, flowing streams, lots of turns and switchbacks, and pilgrims slowly making their way uphill in the light rain. I look out the window, mesmerized. I feel my spirit grow quiet and the Lord speaks to me. I'm hearing that this trip will answer my prayer to be vulnerable and loving, without hesitation, without fear, without looking to be loved in return. That's a tall order, I know.

In the past year I have been listening to podcasts and interviews with several leaders in this exploration. One who really inspires me is Brené Brown, research professor, University of Houston. She has written about and given TED talks on being vulnerable.

Vulnerability. That's a mouthful. Brown says:

> "Owning our story can be hard but not nearly as difficult as spending our lives running from it. Embracing our vulnerabilities is risky but not nearly as dangerous as giving up on love and belonging and joy—the experiences that make us the most vulnerable. Only when we are brave enough to explore the darkness will we discover the infinite power of our light."

–Brené Brown, The Gifts of Imperfection

Watching raindrops fall on pilgrims struggling up the mountain, I reflect on what I've been learning about myself and what I want to change. I have a hard shell of numbness about me. It has begun to crack and I want to crack it more. I want to break it wide open and be free to feel, to be who I really am inside rather than to conform to what I think I should be. Rather than do the things I think I should do.

Again drawing from the wisdom of Brown, I have an inkling on where to start: "Believing that you're enough is what gives you the courage to be authentic."

Can I do that? Can I really come to believe that I am enough?

It's mid-afternoon when the bus leaves me and Amy at the 183-bed *Albergue de Peregrinos (Pilgrim's Hostel)* de Orreaga / Roncesvalles. It's an old convent established in the 12th century when King Alfonso I asked the Bishop of Pamplona to set up the Roncesvalles Hospitality Institution. Its mission was to help pilgrims crossing the Pyrenees along the Camino. Today it is staffed by teams of volunteers from Holland, volunteers who I find to be kind, cheerful and happy to be helping us pilgrims.

Amy and I stake out our beds in a cubicle of two sets of bunk beds. We both take the bottom beds. After a brief rest, I wander around a bit. The rain has stopped; the sun is shining. I join other pilgrims who have moved their hiking shoes from inside to the outside to dry in the sun. Shoes are not allowed in the *albergues*, and I appreciate that. They have shelves where you leave your shoes outside the facility, or just inside the door. That makes sense. I can well imagine what odors might give us nightmares if we leave our shoes bedside the beds.

Pilgrims set shoes out to dry in the sun

I make my way to the adjacent Church of Santa Maria and take a seat on a wooden bench in the back. The lights are dim. Choral music plays softly. Other pilgrims quietly enter, quietly leave. Some also sit on the benches in silence. It's a tender moment and tears stream down my cheeks. Tears for David. I realize I'm beginning to say my final good-bye.

My Camino is the resolution of all that has come, all that was, and all that would be. As I let go my shoulders sink into rest. Tension releases. My mind falls into a meditative state.

Absolution. The word *absolution* comes to me.

In 1179 Pope Alexander III proclaimed that pilgrims who traveled the Camino, performed certain rituals and reached Santiago would receive forgiveness for all sins. Absolution of sin. Many notable figures throughout history, and a great many more unknown pilgrims, have traveled to

Santiago for a variety of reasons. Sometimes they seek absolution.

But me? It's strange that I should think of this. I'm not in need of absolution. I have confidence with my Lord God and am forgiven for any offence I have ever or would ever give. Why absolution?

Suddenly, in the stillness of the dim light, I know. I'm here for me to absolve myself of judgment I hold against me. I'm here to forgive myself; to come to know and love myself and to release myself of guilt.

The awareness grows, the tears increase. I have a strong sense that in these 37 days on the Camino I will accomplish this. I will become free to be my authentic self.

I linger, sitting in silence, in calm. After some time, I regain composure and return to my bunk. Amy and I have purchased the pilgrim's dinner option with our room, and we've been assigned to join a table of twelve in the restaurant. Conversation is engaging as we all talk of where we're from and why we're on the Camino. This is the starter for most conversations we will have over the next month. We all have a story. For me, I realize that story is just beginning to unfold.

Day 2: July 10
Roncesvalles - Vizkarret, 7 miles

Amy and I leave at 6:45 a.m. We dress, put on our shoes and grab our shiny new trekking poles. I had twisted mine to reduce their length the night before, and now can't extend one of them again. It's broken. A man kindly gives it a try but he can't budge it either. I give up, frustrated. I guess one pole will be good enough.

Amy and I both have issues with our feet and feel we will need to walk slowly. However, I quickly learn that my slow is far slower than hers. Less than a half hour into the walk, Amy is out of sight, far ahead of me – on her own pilgrimage. She plans on walking much further today than me. I'm not sure if I'll see her again, but it was nice to have started off together.

I walk alone, often passed by other pilgrims. The sun is high in the sky and wearing me down. I laugh at myself as I recall a scene from my hiking practice back in Indiana where I regularly walked a three-mile trail around Bixler Lake. One day an old man was walking in the distance ahead of me. He was unsteady and he wavered side to side. I was certain he was about to fall over. I quickened my pace to catch up so that I could be at hand and ready to help him. I caught up just as he reached his car. He turned and said hello to me and we chatted a bit. I learned that he was 74 years old and makes this walk every day to stay in shape!

As I journey along the way, on an empty stomach and without much shade, I walk like I had seen him walk. Unsteady, staggering side to side. I feel like I will fall over at any moment. What a sight I must be! Starting the day I had been quite concerned about my Achilles heels, but now every other part of my short little legs vies for my attention – knees, thighs, calves, ankles, hips. I am in pain. The road is a constant long, slow ascent and descent, ascent and descent. The hills just don't end.

Finally, after seven miles I reach Vizkarret. It's 11:00 a.m. and I'm famished, weak and tired. I walk into the local bar, the first one I've passed that is open, and sit down to breakfast – *café con leche* (coffee with milk), fresh squeezed orange juice, and *tortilla española*. Don't be fooled by the name. This *tortilla* is not what we call tortilla in the United States. It is a potato pie, a quiche, and it is absolutely delicious!

The bar in Spain is more like an American coffee shop or restaurant that also sells liquor. It is frequented by families and children, and certainly by tired and hungry pilgrims. I sit at my table inside, cooling off while I eat. I watch several local men gather and laugh, swapping stories and ribbing each other. I'm intrigued.

Then it dawns on me that this region of Spain is Basque country. Graffiti fills many of the walls in the area, stating "No es españa (This is not Spain)." The Basque people have tried to separate from Spain for many years. They have their own dialect, their own culture, their own ways. They would like independence from Spain. I recall when David and I were in Spain in 1997 we avoided the Basque region because there were bombings and attacks of unrest for this reason.

As I watch the men I become keenly aware of David's Basque blood line. I am so taken with how their features are like those of my husband, his father and his brothers. The coloring, shape of the face and clarity of their eyes. The resemblance is profound.

View of the rolling hills from my room.

I decide to stop for the day and treat myself to a private room at Amatxi-Elsa Casa Rural rather than an *albergue* with lots of roommates. A casa rural provides a private bedroom in a home. This was a beautiful home run by a lovely elderly couple originally from Argentina. We talk awhile in Spanish. My Spanish is obviously quite helpful along the Camino. Many of the people – hostel hosts and pilgrims – do speak English, but even more speak Spanish. And I love to speak Spanish!

I began learning the language in 1978 when, as a young 23-year old, I lived in Guadalajara, in the state of Jalisco, Mexico. I lived with a family that didn't speak English – that really facilitated and accelerated my learning.

I still think that is the best way to learn a new language – to be immersed in it. I was there only seven months, but it was enough to give me a foundation to become fluent.

It was also a foundational experience in finding myself – pardon the cliché. Living in Mexico alone, without being surrounded by friends and family who grew up with me, gave me space to just be me. No expectations. No past habits or reputation to live up to. It was a wonderful time, and I think that's where I first stepped into owning my life. I had a sense of adventure that paid off with great experiences, a deeper understanding and appreciation for life, and some lifelong friendships.

I married David five years later. His mother was from Juarez, Mexico and preferred Spanish over English. David was bilingual and had also lived in Guadalajara. Spanish and a love of the culture became a great bond between David and me. We spent a lot of time in Mexico and spent a lot of time among Spanish-speaking friends and family in Los Angeles. Being in Spain now reminds me of how much I love Latin culture and how much I enjoy conversing in Spanish.

Being on this journey also reminds me that I'm brave and adventurous. I didn't think I was. I had become subdued and predictable through my adult years. But repeatedly when friends would hear of my plans to hike the Camino alone this past year, they would comment on how adventurous I am. *No, I'm not* I would think. Then one day someone convinced me otherwise. She reminded me that as a young woman I had gone to Mexico where I didn't speak the language, and where

I lived with strangers. *Okay, I guess I am. I really am adventurous.*

As I check in at the Casa Rural I start to tell the host couple that the men at the bar reminded me of my husband and his father's family; they are Basque.

I get as far as saying, "*Mi marido* (My husband) . . ." and then I begin to sob. I'm surprised, just as surprised as the couple standing in front of me. I cry and they comfort me until finally I can spit it out – "My husband was of Basque ancestry and he died three years ago. That's why I'm walking to Santiago," I share. I didn't see that emotion coming.

Once I get to my room and finish releasing what has been pent up inside, I realize that this is my first entry into being vulnerable. My shell cracked just a little, and it feels good. It also feels scary.

I lay in the afternoon sun and begin reading from a book I downloaded to my iPhone for the trip: *Hinds' Feet on High Places*. I read it in the 70s and I decided to read it again while on this journey. I quickly find out that it coincides perfectly with my Camino experience.

The book was written in 1955 by Hannah Hurnard. It's an allegory of how Much Afraid (the young protagonist of the story) is transformed from being a doubtful, crippled woman living in the Valley of Fear to a confident, bold woman climbing in the High Places. Its title is taken from Bible scripture, Habakkuk 3:19 which says,

"The Lord God is my strength, and he will make my feet like hinds' feet, and he will make me to walk upon mine high places."

The story strikes me as intensive spiritual therapy for Much Afraid . . . as is the Camino for me. She goes from walking in the Valley of Fear to walking with God on the High Places of Joy. It's not an easy path. Not at all. Yet her inner growth seems to make the suffering worth the hardships. I suspect that's what lays ahead for me on this trek.

CHAPTER 3

Oh, the People You Meet

Day 3: July 11
Vizkarret – Illaratz, 8 miles

I make a leisurely departure at 9:00 a.m. for my eight-mile walk to Illaratz where I've made reservations for tonight. My hosts send me off with the most common phrase heard over the next month, *Buen camino,* or *Safe travel.* Literally translated *good path or way*, it is a greeting spoken when passing pilgrims on the road. It connotes a bond, a knowing, and well wishes.

The running of the rams

Walking alone through the countryside on the outskirts of town, I'm deep in thought when I hear a bell ringing. I turn to look behind me. A herd of rams are coming my way – filling the breadth of the road and leaving nowhere for me to escape to. I turn sideways and press my body up against the brush lining the path. As the herd runs past, one brushes my leg. It's a scary moment, but at the same time I find it humorous. This very same week is the Festival of St. Fermin in Pamplona, just a day's walk ahead. The festival highlight is the famous Running of the Bulls. So while I won't run with the bulls, I guess I can say I did run with the rams.

Today's walk is a challenge once again. Hills and heat, and occasional shade. This is peppered with some very nice visits with other pilgrims. That's the kind of experience the Camino is about in large degree. *Oh, the people you will meet.* People from around the world, with varied lives, walking through the same physical hardships to reach the same destination.

I finish the downhill slope of a tricky narrow path to find a van anchored as a roadside stand, forming a shade. Its entrepreneur is selling drinks and snacks. It's very timely. There are tables and chairs and umbrellas scattered around. I buy a lemonade and take an empty seat among some enthusiastic young people. We introduce ourselves and I learn they're from South Korea. They ask why I'm on the Camino.

Me? I'm here because my husband died. I was single 30 years, married about 30 years, and now I'm looking at what to do with my next 30 years. That's my story. I'll tell it many times over the next month.

I can see that my young friends are impressed that I'm making this pilgrimage alone and at my age. I see they're even more impressed that I'm from Los Angeles, home of the Los Angeles Dodgers. One shares that he hopes to one day travel to America to see them play. His friend also wants to go to Los Angeles, but his goal is to see the L.A. Lakers. They are refreshing. Their energy is contagious. I leave feeling revived and ready for more.

At another break a few hours later, shaded under a thatched roof in a set of buildings of a small settlement, I meet Shannon. She's from Modesto, California. She's in her last year of a Master's program, studying Social Science at a university in Spain. She doesn't know what's next. What path will she take? She's walking the Camino looking for direction.

At the same stop I am entertained by five Irish men who are walking the Camino as a fundraiser for a nonprofit which provides mentoring for disadvantaged youth. Learning of my background work with nonprofits, they invite me to come to Ireland and do an apprenticeship with them. That's an intriguing idea, I think. They are a lively and fun group. I wish I could walk fast enough to keep step with them. I enjoy their teasing and bantering with one another, but I know I can't keep up with them.

Meeting fellow pilgrims like this makes the walk easier. It takes my attention off the pains in my body and places it on human connection. I am touched at the many reasons for which people are putting themselves out, challenging their physicality, endurance and mental stamina. The Camino endears itself to me all the more, knowing that although I'm walking alone, it is not in isolation. We have a shared spirit and experience on the road.

As I continue up the trail, I tear up again. This time because I'm acutely aware that God loves me so much. He shows it through all his creation. The people and the flowers and rocks and trees. Walking through narrow trails, I imagine that the plants are lined up with high fives. I hear them saying "You go, girl! You got this! You can do it." I suspect they may even know my name.

Day 4: July 12
Illaratz – Cizur Menor, 13 miles (3 by bus)

I was the only pilgrim to stay at *Albergue Aca y Alla* (This and That Hostel) last night. Strange. They tell me seven stayed here the night before. You never know what to expect.

I can tell my host is anxious for me to get on my way as I finish my morning *café con leche* and toast. He's dressed in white shirt, white pants, and with a red bandana around his neck. The traditional wear for the Festival de San Fermin. He says that he's driving to Pamplona to party today. Festivities have been going on every day this week. When he tells me it's just a twenty-minute drive, I'm tempted to ask to hitch a ride with him. My walk to Pamplona will take me all day! I resist.

I'm on my way by 7:30 a.m., enjoying a crisp and clear morning. The road takes me uphill – up, up, up until I reach an ancient church building. I stop and rest for a moment, then go down, down, down the other side. My body hurts in so many different places and my thighs are *coming to life* in a way I have never ever before felt.

I begin to mentally calculate how many days I've been walking now – one, two, three . . . oh, three days! I'm only starting on my fourth day. Feels like so many more!

It's strange that no pilgrims are passing me this morning. It's really quiet. I appreciate the solitude. On the downside of the hill I meet a local walking toward me. We stop and chat. What nice weather today. How beautiful the sky is. Where am I from? Am I going all the way to Santiago? Then out of nowhere he informs me, "This is not the Camino."

"No?" Evidently I've ventured off the path.

"But keep going," he says. "You'll cross the path just a little further down the road." We laugh.

"Buen camino," he says as I thank him and continue on down, with my one pole helping to slow me down and ease pressure on my knees. I make it to the road below and realize the main path was alongside the paved road – a nice level walk. Now I see pilgrims trekking along on with ease and energy which seems to always flourish in the early morning hours. *Oh well, I guess I needed the exercise*, I think to myself.

From here though, the path once again begins to wave up and down, up and down. The hills are relentless. Saving grace is that the path now winds below some tree covered sections. Cooling me. Calming my heart. Inspiring me with beautiful vistas.

A few hours later I come to a small café. Several pilgrims are seated at the outside patio. I go inside and order a zucchini quiche and fresh squeezed orange juice, then join the others. We talk and we laugh. I share with them about the detour I had mistakenly taken this morning and ask that they keep an eye on me or no telling where I'll end up.

Sure enough, just a half hour after leaving them I hear the high school teacher from New York who I had just met call out to me, "It's this way." Ooops, I've missed the yellow arrow marking a narrow path. Quickly I turn around and jump into file behind her, thankful for the course correction. We walk together for a short distance and then her pace leaves me behind. At least I'm on the right path! I think about how wonderful it is to be looked after and to look out for others . . . to be a part of community.

I think about this week being Festival de Fermin, which means it's time for Pamplona's famous *running of the bulls*. That should be exciting news, but the idea of seeing the bull run is pre-empted by finding out that there is no lodging available in the city – at least not at a reasonable cost. They say there will be a million visitors in Pamplona this week. That makes me worry a little about my safety. After some investigation I make a reservation at the hostel in Cizur Menor on the other side of Pamplona. That will mean walking at least 13 miles on a very, very hot day. Most pilgrims walk 12 – 16 miles a day, but that's quite a challenge for me. A young couple share with me that they will take a bus from Villava, a suburb of Pamplona, to get through the city and its thousands of visitors. I decide to do the same.

I'm exhausted when I reach Villava. I get directions and board the bus to Pamplona city center, about three miles away. I'm so embarrassed. Everyone on the bus, and throughout the city for that matter, is dressed in white with red bandanas, the traditional festival dress. Then comes this short, tired pilgrim in green tank top and black shorts and hefty backpack to squeeze into the bus among them. I can feel

41

the stares. They know that pilgrims are supposed to walk, not ride a bus. I look down, avoiding eye contact.

I get off in city center where I need to transfer to another bus. There are throngs of people. It's really hot and I'm really tired. I unload my pack and take off my shoes to rest on a small patch of grass I've found in the middle of the cement thoroughfare. I wish I could score a seat in the shade but none are available, so I sit in the sun and enjoy an orange juice and half of a turnover I bought at a nearby store.

After regaining some strength, I decide to walk the rest of the way. It's only three more miles. I figure I can do that. Maybe I'm also wanting to avoid the judgmental stares on another bus. It's now 3:00 in the afternoon, under direct sun, in 89-degree heat. It's easy-going for the first mile and I feel proud of myself. Slowly, the next mile turns into a torturous struggle.

Walking on asphalt through a city has to be the worst of the Camino. If I were walking down a farm road or through a lovely forested area, I would be fine. But this city walking is doubly, triply tiring. And following the markers is more difficult – they're often hard to spot on the sidewalks. Half of the time I'm unsure if I'm still on the path. Maybe I missed a turn. Then at the last moment, as I consider retracing my steps, I come across another marker or see another pilgrim ahead of me and know I'm going in the right direction.

As I get to the outer edge of the city a pair of fellow pilgrims stop to help me pull my water bottle out of my backpack. I'm dehydrated, I'm sure. I carry my water in a side pocket on my backpack, but the pack is so full that the bottle is pushed just out of reach. I have to take the backpack off to reach the water. That's why I haven't been drinking much of it. The two women are visibly concerned about me – sweaty and weary and exhausted. They're reluctant to leave me, but I'm embarrassed to hold them back. I assure them I'll be okay, though I'm not sure of that myself. I'm refreshed with the water and have only one mile to go. They move on ahead.

I drag myself the remaining mile to my hostel, arriving around 5:30. I sign in and make my way to my assigned room. As I turn the corner into the courtyard, *L.A. Dodger* and *L.A. Laker* (as I've come to think of them) come running to greet me with big hugs and smiles, shouting, "You made it!" I'm so sweaty and smelly that I'm embarrassed as I hug them. They are so sweet and they genuinely are happy to see me. I suspect they may have doubted if I was really up to the physical challenge and that's why they're excited that I really did make it. It's good to see them and the other young South Koreans I had met yesterday.

Keeping the pilgrim routine, I shower, hand wash my clothes, and hang them on the clothes line to dry. Each day that's what I do. It's a necessity with just two sets of clothes. Upon arrival, you shower, put on clean clothes and wash the dirty, smelly ones you just took off. You hang them on the line and hope they dry by bedtime. Sometimes a hostel has laundry service and you can pay for them to wash and dry them in machines and I do take advantage of that from time to time. But not today. And today I've arrived so late that my socks don't get dry. Luckily, I brought three pair with me and so I do have a dry set for tomorrow.

Around 7:00 I'm hungry, I pull a banana from my backpack that I bought this morning. I'm glad it's still edible because I'm *just too damn tired to go find dinner*. My feet hurt too much. I visit a little with my South Korean friends, and then with Rob and Emma, a young couple from Ireland. We talk about blisters as they doctor theirs. I see that I have a small one wanting to come up on my toe, and Emma gives me some Compeed to stop it before it can take hold.

Sixteen of us are sleeping in a room of bunk beds. There are three other rooms equally filled. I try to rest a while, but it's hot inside. There's no air conditioning or breeze. What troubles me even more is that the paper mattress covers they gave us are noisy. I put mine on the bed and then unrolled my sleeping bag liner on top of it. Every time I move, turning from one side to the other or just readjusting my body, the paper cover crinkles and makes noise. It's not just me. I hear the sound throughout the room as others try to rest – and it continues all through the night.

I think about what I'm learning through this experience. Today's journal entry reads:

"Just keep going.

"Today I wore my wide brim hat in the blazing sun along narrow paths going uphill. If I lifted my head I would see the trail just goes up and up with no end in sight. It's discouraging. It was better to keep my head down, eyes on the path at

44

my feet, and not worry over how far it would wind uphill. I was going to have to walk it regardless, so why look ahead and create dread?

"This was a very difficult day for me physically, but in the end, I made it. Days like this contribute to the overall growing sense that *I can do anything.*"

I smile as I read from *Hinds Feet on High Places*. Seems that Much Afraid is having a day a lot like mine. Getting to the High Places of Joy is no easy matter.

Day 5: July 13
Cizur Menor – Zariquiequi, 3.6 miles

Today's a short 3.6 mile walk to Albergue San Andres in Zariquiequi. I cautiously – over cautiously – decide to make it a short one to rest up in preparation for tomorrow's more strenuous climb.

I start out passing through the most beautiful fields of sunflowers. Happy sunflowers. Smiling faces. I love their energy.

Walking alongside fields of sunflowers

Christian, a handsome young man from Italy, slows his pace and walks with me. This is his fifth Camino. He has done the Portuguese trail twice, English once and now this is his second time on the French way. We talk about what people are looking for from the Camino.

"You have to ask good questions," he says. "That's the key. You have to ask the right questions. Answers will come based on the questions you ask."

I agree. As he bids me *buen camino* and moves on ahead at his faster pace, I ponder the idea. It's not new to me.

In the past few years I've been encouraged with the teachings of spiritual leader and author Michael Bernard Beckwith. He talks about visioning our lives and living our true potential. He talks about the universe answering our questions. The key is to ask the right questions. Ask questions that empower us and avoid those that disempower us. Empowerment comes from questions like, "What's trying to emerge in my life?". . . "What is my purpose?". . . "What gifts do I have to give the world?" Those questions create a powerful, positive force for change.

Questions such as "What's wrong?" and "Why me?" are disempowering. They lock us into a downward spiral and keep us in a negative and limited state, feeling like victims.

So I've been learning to ask questions. I think this Camino is part of my answer.

In January, just six months before leaving for Spain, I attended a three-day *Dream Builder Live* seminar with Mary Morrissey, life coach, spiritual leader and author. What I experienced further solidified what I had been learning and pursuing in my spiritual life. It helped me to create a blueprint to really open up to life and manifest my dreams – starting with learning what those dreams are. I dare say my commitment to hike the Camino may have not materialized if I had not experienced those three days in that Los Angeles hotel, getting inspired along with 900 fellow sojourners. I left with confidence and a better understanding of my life, the spirit, and my purpose. I left with a stronger commitment to hike the Camino.

Like Beckwith, Morrissey emphasized the importance of asking high quality questions. Again, I heard that the universe will answer the questions that we ask. All too often our questions have nothing to do with what we truly seek, truly desire. We deny ourselves, too afraid to voice our desires, afraid we are unworthy of them. Too often our attention (and therefore the universe's response) focuses on what we don't have, what's gone wrong, and we leave it at that. We settle for less and never reach our true purpose. We never even come to know what it is.

Perhaps that's a story to share another day. Meanwhile, in the middle of my Camino, out of nowhere, Christian has appeared with the same message, to raise my awareness once again.

But what do I ask? What is my question? I don't know.

I wish I could keep up with Christian to continue the conversation, but I can't. I'm the slow pilgrim. My short little legs just don't move me along very fast. I think I can substantiate scientifically that I'm the slowest. I've never passed anyone else on the trail. They always pass me. I guess that's okay, it makes room for quiet thought. It gives me opportunity to contemplate what questions to ask of the Camino, because I still don't know.

Time passes quickly. I get to my hostel early; settle in, shower and wash clothes – all before noon. So I sit at the sidewalk café attached to my hostel, drinking coffee and watching pilgrims enter and pass through town. Most just keep going, finding it too early to stop for the day.

Agnes from Poland joins me for lunch. At the next table a man from Brazil tells us that he was in a lot of pain on his walk yesterday. He demonstrates how he walked – slowly shifting leg to leg, sideways, barely moving forward. I recognize that! It's the way I start out in the mornings. Then a young man from France gets up from another table to go inside. He walks the same way. We're all in stitches as we laugh in solidarity and knowing: It's the Pilgrim's Walk!

Still sitting outside in the afternoon, I meet 68-year old Antonio. He lives in Pamplona. He rode his bicycle, as he often does, the seven miles to this town to visit the hostel staff and to chat up the pilgrims – pilgrims like me. He is so proud of me for doing this at my age. He shares his wisdom with me.

First, he tells me to use trekking poles – two of them. I've been using just one pole since my second one broke the first day of the hike. It helps a lot when going uphill and equally when going down steep declines. It helps me to balance. Antonio makes a good case for why I should use two, so I make a mental note to buy a second one as soon as I run across a store that sells them. (Note: I did that a few days later in Estella, and it was a big help.)

Secondly, he tells me to send my backpack by "taxi" each day to take the weight off my back and save me from strain on my knees. Even though my pack is only about 17 pounds, it adds up day in and day out.

Tomorrow's hike is a steep climb so I decide to take Antonio's advice and make arrangements with my host. I pay 5 euros to have my backpack transported from here to my next hostel. I check my guidebook and call a hostel to make reservations for tomorrow and to make sure they can receive the bag.

I decide that I'll do this on days when the terrain will be difficult. For the most part, I like carrying my backpack. I feel proud to hoist it onto my back. It's part of the experience. On the other hand, my goal is to finish the Camino and this may be a small physical adjustment that can help me to reach that goal.

Day 6: July 14
Zariquieui – Obanos, 6 miles

My feet enjoyed a good rest yesterday, but I had a horrible sleepless night. It was so, so hot in the hostel. The man sleeping next to the outer wall shut the window. I was so sweaty and I got preoccupied with bed bugs. Got a little welt on my arm (a mosquito bite) but it got my mind racing about bed bugs—something I've read about and feared. I'm very happy to climb out of my bunk and head out on the road bright and early.

It's so cold and windy on this stretch, and my fleece jacket has gone ahead in my backpack. I didn't realize I should have held on to it since the previous days had been so hot. Today the trail ascends to an altitude of 2600 feet, leveling off at *Alto de Perdón* (Place of Forgiveness).

As I start up the path, my heart grows heavy. It gently whispers to my mind what it is I have to do today. I'm angry about it. *I do not want to walk up this %*#! damn camino,* I think to myself, fuming. I let the anger pour out. Slowly I ascend both the mountain and the anger.

At the top is a sculptural depiction of pilgrims through the years making their way west on the Camino. In the background, wind turbines from the next hill tower over them. I try to protect myself from the harsh and very cold wind. My long sleeve shirt isn't enough, but it's all I have. I regret that I sent my bag with my fleece jacket ahead by taxi. The wind is loud and relentless. I sit on the ledge of a cement monument, let tears run down my face, and I forgive David. I forgive him for dying and leaving me alone.

I'm surprised. I didn't know that was in me. I thought I was past losing him. When he had told me that he was tired of being so sick and wanted to go, I had told him he could go and I would be okay. I thought I would, and I was for a couple of years. Now I realize it wasn't true. It was a lie I told myself. Now I'm coming to terms with it. I feel such a heavy weight lift from me.

Right on cue, Rob and Emma arrive when my tears subside. I share with Rob that I've just forgiven my husband for dying and leaving me. I feel it's necessary to say this aloud to someone, and they're the ones who show up. Rob says that he is touched that I would share such an intimate thing, and he thanks me. We talk a little and I become aware of how healing it is to share this experience with other souls. It feels very much like a needful part of the process.

In 1996 Vicente Galbete created this set of sculptures dedicated to the Pilgrim's Way. It is called *Where the way of the wind meets the way of the stars*. It represents pilgrims from different eras of the camino walks.

The descent from *Alto de Perdón* is a long hard climb over loose stone. It is slow and challenging, but I feel great. I do a roll call of body parts – they all check in and report that they are fine. My feet don't even hurt – a rarity on the trail. My wanna-be blister that was treated with the Compeed Emma had given me, is gone. Life is wonderful.

I pick up two small stones as I walk out of the cold windy hills into the valley. I add one to a man-made altar to the side of the rocky path. There are several stones on it. I tell

God that I do trust him and lay down this stone as a physical action to remember that, and to know that I don't need to carry burdens. I put the other in my pocket and figure I'll know what to do with it later.

By the time I get down from the mountain and to the next town the sun is in full force. Sweaty, tired and yet excited, I walk by a bar where some pilgrims – 20 something year olds from Spain, Germany, Austria and New Zealand, and a middle-aged woman from Japan are seated in the shade outside. They invite me to join them for a beer and I do. It's so energizing to laugh, tease and swap stories.

An hour or so later I check into my hostel, shower and do laundry. I walk to the town square and sit on a bench in the park. I had wanted a bite to eat, but it's Sunday and everything is closed.

I sit in the shade and there's a nice breeze blowing. I take off my shoes, as I do any chance I get, and rest them on the soft green grass. It's heavenly. I admire the use of colorful flowers in the homes surrounding the square. In traditional Spanish style, red and pink peak out from boxes lining the second story windows. I grow to appreciate this more and more along the trail. That, and the rounded arches that grace beautiful entry ways into humble homes. Entry ways that are also bordered by rich earthen orange pots of colorful flowers.

It's been a very full and very good day. I finish it off with dinner at a bar around the corner, watching the bull fights on a large screen TV. The room is filled with the locals.

I enjoy watching them cheer the matadors and make the most of the last day of the Festival of San Fermin.

Once back in the hostel I fall asleep with a thankful heart.

CHAPTER 4

He will make my feet like hinds' feet,
leaping on mountains and skipping on hills.

Day 7: July 15
Obanos – Lorca, 8.5 miles

Alas, the thankful heart doesn't last. The heat has intensified. Lots of very steep uphill climbs on dirt passages make it even worse. I feel like crying. In fact, I do cry! I ask God why he would bring me here.

In response, what I hear is that he wants to show me I'm stronger than I think and he's making my feet like hinds' feet. The Good Shepherd in *Hinds Feet on High Places* shares with Much Afraid the joy of having hinds' feet: ". . . and like a young hart or a roebuck I can go leaping on the mountains and skipping on the hills with the greatest ease and pleasure."

But me? Today I'm not buying it. I'm not so keen on finding out if I'm stronger than I think. I'm not so sure that I want feet like hinds' feet. I mean, after all, *How much more strength do I need?* I like to be comfortable. I want an easy path.

I struggle on through the dirt. I feel weak. The thought occurs to me that I'm probably dehydrated. I could pass out.

If I do, who knows how long it would be before anyone would find me. I keep moving on, one step in front of the other. What else can I do?

At 2:30 I get to Lorca, dragging myself down the dusty street through the middle of town. It's quiet. No one is outside. I arrive at Albergue Lorca and they immediately

Hot, dusty, and dehydrated. I keep going.

give me water and tell me to sit down. Then after a brief rest, the hostess leads me to a room on the first floor, commenting that she doesn't think I can make it to the second floor. I don't either. I'm thankful to climb up only one flight of stairs. (Note: What they call the first floor in Spain is the first one up from the ground floor.) I'm exhausted, mentally and physically. As soon as I get in my room I start crying. These are tears of exhaustion, and they continue to flow as I shower.

I wash my clothes and hang them on a pole that stretches out from my window, . . . over the street below. That's right. My underwear is hanging over the streets of Lorca, like a flag. That gives me a little laugh and my mood lightens.

The day's cry is out of my system by the time I meet my roommate – John, a high school teacher from Canada. It seems strange that I'm sleeping alone in a room with a man I don't know. But I hardly give it a second thought. In the same situation in the United States I would protest, of course. I would feel uncomfortable. But this is just the way it is on the Camino. I feel perfectly safe and no longer think anything of it.

John and I have dinner downstairs in the small dining area of the hostel. It's so hot, I'm not very hungry. I opt for just a salad. I enjoy the conversation with John who is making the trek on his bicycle. As we talk I forget my woes.

Day 8: July 16
Lorca – Azqueta, 10 miles

The next day brings no relief. John leaves before sunrise to escape some of the heat. He's left a paper in the middle of the floor wishing me "Buen camino." *That's sweet*, I think to myself.

I don't leave until there is some light outside, around 6:45 a.m. I stop in Estella for breakfast and a quick stop in a store to buy a trekking pole to replace the one I had broken. I don't hang around too long because I know it's going to get really hot and I want to get as far as I can.

The rolling red hills and vineyards frame the trail as I leave Estella, but there's no shade. I don't even dally for long when I reach the famed Irache wine fountain where pilgrims fill their water bottles with wine, for free, compliments of the *Bodegas Irache*. I empty the water out of my bottle, then pull the fountain's lever to put a little red wine in it. I don't want much, only a swallow to taste it and say I drank some. It's really way too hot to be drinking wine.

I rinse the bottle, refill it with water and turn back on the road. A man is passing by and calls out to me to not drink the wine, it's too hot. I assure him I'm not drinking it, and he comes over and continues to chat. We're alone. No one else is around, and for the first (and only) time on the road I feel uncomfortable. I end the conversation and try to leave, but not quickly enough.

"Your backpack sits too low," he tells me in Spanish. "You need to get the weight off your back," and at the same time he reaches out and pulls the straps to tighten it, bringing the pack way up on my shoulders (where it should not be). I don't argue. I quickly say thank you, and move away and down the road. Whew! I escape what I think could have been a problem.

A short ways further I stop under a shade to pull out my water for a drink. I can't. I can't get the pack off. My backpack is so tight it's like a straightjacket. I can't loosen the straps or pull my arms through the holes. "Don't panic," I tell myself. "Worst case scenario is that I will have to ask for help when someone comes along and passes me. And for sure, someone will pass by." In the end, it didn't come to that. I finally inched it off bit by bit, drank my water, and loosened the straps before putting it back on, positioning it for my hips to take the weight, as it should be.

It's super hot now, almost unbearable. I feel angry. I talk to God and all I get is that it's easy to be loving and feel so thankful when circumstances are good and I'm in control. But here in the middle of nowhere I have no control. It sucks. I'm mad.

I think this is a Camino lesson. I'm not in control. Nope. The Camino is in charge, leading me step by step, moment by moment. I don't know what's coming ahead. I just follow the yellow arrows marking the way, up and down, over and under, on smooth ground, hard ground, over loose rock and endless dirt surfaces with no end in sight. I just keep walking. This path has a destination, but I don't know what it is.

It's hard to not be in control. I'm starting to realize what a control freak I am. I feel so vulnerable – and it's an uncomfortable feeling. When I started the Camino I was impressed with the need to be vulnerable. I think about the bus ride over the Pyrenees and welcoming the warm thought of learning to be open and vulnerable. It's no longer a warm thought. It's irritating, to say the least. Today I really am vulnerable. I think on that as I continue to walk. Me and Much Afraid; we're both vulnerable. We're both learning to trust.

While I complain I also realize that I'm getting to know the Camino as a trusted friend. Despite my bitching, I'm aware that I'm in the middle of a healing union of mind, spirit and body. I'm developing a vague concept that these physical hardships of walking the Camino are connected to something in my soul, in my spirit. I think it can only be accessed when I'm at the end of my physical strength. I don't quite understand, but I know there's something to it. I suppose – I hope – it will unfold as I continue.

At 2:00 I arrive at my hostel with a big blister on the bottom of my left foot. It's on my arch and it spreads over the edge and to the side of my foot. *Like I need something more to complain about*, I think as I look at it. Before leaving home I had read a lot about how to avoid blisters and if you don't avoid them, and most pilgrims don't, how to treat them using a needle and thread. I brought needle and thread with me, just in case. I had so hoped I would be one of the few pilgrims who make the full trip without any blisters. I guess I won't be. I've got a big one.

Using a needle and thread to drain the blister scares me. You're supposed to thread the needle, push it through the blister and out the other side and cut the thread, leaving strands hanging at each end. This is enough to give the fluid buildup an escape route. It's daunting to me.

At the hostel, once again there is only one other pilgrim staying the night. His name is Allessio. While I'm talking with the hostess, checking to see if I'm really understanding what to do about this blister, Allessio steps over. He offers me a patch to put over it. He had bought a package of them before leaving for the trip but hadn't used one yet. You're supposed to cover the blister and not touch it, he tells me. Let it drain on its own. That sounds better than poking it with a needle, so I thank him and the three of us gather around my foot to try it out. Allesio gives me an extra one in case I need it later.

There it is again, I think. *Another pilgrim looking out for me.* I remember the young man who helped me the first night of my trip, when I arrived in St. Jean Pied de Port in the rain and lost. He helped me find my hostel. "That's what we do," he said when I thanked him. "We look out for one another."

Over dinner I learn that Allessio is a Catholic priest. He's been serving in Mozambique the past ten years and now the church has called him to return to Italy, his birthplace. When he finishes the Camino he will begin a new mission.

Wisely, the bishop told him to take the summer to walk the Camino as a transition from one country to the other, one mindset, one culture, one lifestyle, to a new one. I appreciate the journey before him. This certainly can't be easy for him. It's clear to me that he loves Mozambique and didn't want to leave. Like me, I imagine he's had quite a few poignant conversations with God.

I climb into my bed, into my sleeping bag liner in a hot room. I have an open window near me, but there is no breeze. I feel sad, mad and emotionally spent. I've heard that the first days can be quite difficult on the Camino. I lay silent, hoping I will turn a corner in the coming days and that it will get easier.

I read from *Hinds' Feet on High Places*, to see what's new with Much Afraid. I find the Good Shepherd introduces her to her two traveling companions who will help her climb the mountain. Their names are Sorrow and Suffering.

"I can't go with them," Much Afraid says to the shepherd. "Why do you send them? Couldn't you have given me Joy and Peace to go with me? To encourage me?" She bursts into tears.

Exactly! I think to myself. I had imagined making this pilgrimage with Joy and Peace. But instead I seem to have Sorrow and Suffering dogging me. Much Afraid's journey is my journey -- every step of the way.

Day 9: July 17
Azqueta – Los Arcos, 9.5 miles

Streets are empty in early mornings.

I leave at daybreak without breakfast, not even a cup of coffee. The host says there's a mobile station where I can eat on the way, about two miles down the road. I pass the place, but as I near it, the door opens and a man sticks his head out. He tells me they're closed. So I walk . . . stumble . . . drag . . . a full 9.5 miles to the next town. It's still early and the streets are empty when I reach Los Arcos. I get to the plaza in the middle of town and sit at an outside table for my standard *café con leche*, orange juice and croissant. It tastes so good. I take off my shoes and rest my feet.

I cried again on the road this morning. I'm keenly aware that I don't trust God. Despite what I say and think, I really do not trust God. Just to think – I knew without doubt that he was guiding me to walk this Camino. I knew it was important for me. I had looked forward to it for months. But now a week into the journey, I'm not finding much joy in it; no bursts of enlightenment. I'm constantly teetering on the edge of anger. I have bouts of bitter complaints every day.

Trust God? As I walked down from *Alto de Perdón* a few days ago, I picked up a small stone and set it on a rock altar that someone had started to the side of the trail. As I set my rock in place I said in my heart, *"I do trust you, Lord. This rock represents that I trust you."* Now two days later I'm wondering what that was about. I believed it when I said it, but it's obviously not true. This is a very emotional journey.

Meanwhile, reality is that I still have a big blister on my foot and I'm not convinced my bandage is going to take care of it. It's coming loose. I go to a pharmacy and ask if they have anyone who can help me to pop and drain it. They don't, but the woman at the counter is kind. She directs me to a medical clinic.

At the clinic a nurse takes a look and tells me that they don't recommend opening and draining blisters. The risk for infection is too great. Instead, she puts a special medicated bandage over it – similar to what Allessio had given me. This bandage is larger and will cover it more fully. She tells me to leave it in place and give the body opportunity to re-absorb the fluid without opening the skin. I thank her, pay my $30 bill, and return to my room at a hostel that has been taken over by two dozen young German university students.

Sitting on my bed, slowly I begin to think about God and all that I'm feeling about him. I'm not angry any longer. I meditate. I feel that God is jumping in and walking with me, with compassion for me and for the huge blister on my foot. He is not folding his arms scolding me, saying that I am reaping what I've sown. That I should have done this or done that. This is the thinking that would have filled my mind in times past. I would have been looking for the reason this is happening to me. I would have been looking for where to put blame. But not now. I no longer see God that way. I have a new peace.

Neither is God distant, at the top of the next hill saying, "Come on, you can do it." No, he's not distant from me. He's sitting right next to me, suffering with me, feeling my pain. And with that I begin to feel everything is okay. It really is.

Hungry now, I return to the plaza and order pizza, expecting a single slice. But I'm served a full pizza! So I turn to a table behind me and offer to share. The two couples accept and pull out a chair for me to join them. I'm happy to have the company. I learn that one couple is from the United States, the other – John and Vicki - are from Ireland. They are especially kind and helpful.

When they hear about the trouble I'm having with my heels, Vicki introduces me to another woman at a nearby table who's also having trouble walking. The woman shares that to continue the Camino, she walks part way and then takes the bus when she needs to.

The bus? You can do that? I'm all ears as I talk with my fellow ailing pilgrim. I look at the huge blister still swelling over the bottom of my left foot, I think about the heel pain that is not getting any better, and I ask for directions on how to catch the bus tomorrow.

Day 10: July 18
Los Arcos – Logroño (via bus)

The bus. Yes, I bus from Los Arcos to Logroño, a university city with a population of about 155,000. I consult my guidebook and choose a hotel with a pilgrim's rate for tonight. The pedestrian setting on my iPhone maps app guide me from the bus station. It's a fairly easy walk through typical busy city streets.

In 20 minutes I'm at my hotel and am told they don't have a pilgrim rate. This is going to cost me more than I want to pay, but I don't want to look any further. I want to get off my feet so I give them my credit card and check in.

I spend the afternoon hobbling around the Plaza del Mercado (Market Place). Before returning to my room, I backtrack to Mango, a store I had passed on my way in. I want to buy a pair of pants. I've brought with me a pair that zip off into shorts – very practical – and a pair of light weight black shorts. The shorts are good on hot afternoons through the hillsides, but they are very short. They rise up uncomfortably when I sit and leave me feeling very self-conscious and embarrassed. Plus, in the mornings they do nothing to protect me from the cold. Traveling on the bus today I wore my shawl over my shorts, wrapped like a skirt. I do the same when I enter a church building. Some guidebooks suggest this and it makes sense to me as a sign of respect, and it increases my comfort level.

My shawl has turned out to be very practical on the Camino. It can wrap around my shoulders for warmth, over my head for sun protection, around my waist for a skirt. I've even begun to use it as my towel to dry off after a shower. I left the towel I brought with me at a hostel along the way. A true pilgrim, I'm always looking for ways to lighten my pack. Most hostels have a box of discarded belongings that pilgrims have left for the same reason. They're up for grabs. Giving my shawl one more duty and discarding my towel helped, but now here I am looking to buy another garment that will add that weight back.

I find a decent pair of gray pants, loose fitting with an elastic waist I can pull easily over my shorts in the mornings. I take my purchase and head to the plaza to eat something before returning to my room. I join a trio of teachers from Ireland – three women walking the Camino for summer break. We share in the usual conversations, laugh a bit, and then they head on.

Me? I'm back in my room . . . feet up. I'm increasingly concerned that I not push them beyond repair. I've been told that if the tendons get too damaged, they'll require surgery. I don't want that, but I don't want to stop my pilgrimage either.

Pilgrimage . . . This doesn't seem like a pilgrimage now that I'm in a nice hotel room. I wrestle with the idea that maybe it's a mistake to stay here. The comfort with real bath towels and big bed in an air-conditioned room is relaxing, but it emotionally pulls me off the Camino. I feel like a tourist. I don't feel spiritual – whatever that's supposed to feel like.

I get a sense again of this concept forming in my mind. It's the idea that the difficulty of walking the Camino pulls you into a heart space that you can't access while sitting in the comfort of a modern hotel room. I feel my pilgrimage interrupted. I'm distracted. At the same time, I welcome the rest. And my feet thank me.

Day 11: July 19
Logroño – Azofra 3.6 miles (plus bus)

After some internal conflict and debate, I decide to take the bus again. Today I'll ride 18 miles to Najera.

What a beautiful, glorious ride! I'm on a modern commercial bus with comfortable seats and air conditioning. I know I've really scored today as I look out the window across the hot, dry plain. I appreciate that I'm not in that heat. And more than that, I appreciate that 1970s Spanish music is blaring on the sound system—*Sin Ti* by Los Panchos, *Esta Triste Guitarra* by Emmanuel, and more. This is the soundtrack to my days in Guadalajara. I'm moved to tears, this time for joy as I'm transported back to 1978 and my beloved Mexico. I'm disappointed when we reach Najera so quickly. I'd like much more than a mere thirty minutes on this bus. I would easily ride for hours, but I can't. The Camino calls.

I find an outdoor café along the Najera River for lunch. A group of four are just finishing their meal at the next table. I strike up a conversation with Debbie who is from England but now lives in Spain. She invites me to walk to Azofra with them, just another 3 1/2 miles. She insists. "You can have dinner with us and the rest of our group tonight. You shouldn't stay here alone," she tells me. "There's a nice hostel in Azofra." She knows because she's walked the Camino before.

I hesitate, sharing that I can't walk as fast as they do. "No problem," they say. I finally agree to go with them with the understanding that they should not feel obligated to wait for me. They should go on ahead and not hold back on my account.

I finish my lunch and we start down the dusty road together. True to their word, they don't hold back for me.

They're out of sight in less than thirty minutes. I pick up my pace to try to catch up, or at least keep within eye sight. It's no use. I can't move any faster. It's 90 degrees. There's no shade. I walk alone, and I feel alone.

I don't see Debbie and her group again until dinner time. We meet at a restaurant in town. They're a large group of just over a dozen pilgrims from different countries and of different ages. They clearly have bonded like family. They separate as they walk throughout the day, but meet up for dinner each night. I feel like an outsider, and that's a recurring theme – I just can't find my place.

Tonight the town is celebrating. It's party central and the music blasts into the wee hours of the morning; at least until 1:00. That could be exciting, but it's not. The hostel closes at 10:00 p.m. and locks the gate. We are actually locked in! What if there's an emergency? I think to myself. Tonight it is especially annoying because we can hear the music, the laughter and the party. It's just down the street, but we can't enjoy it. We're locked in!

This isn't the first place I've stayed where I've silently questioned the practice of locking us in. Is it for our safety? I begin to suspect that maybe it's an agreement the hostels make with the towns people. Maybe they lock us in at 10 pm so the locals can have their socializing without the intrusion of strangers. So they can own their streets. Maybe.

I know from my 1997 trip to Spain that the Spanish are very sociable. The whole family often strolls about town in the evening, late evening. They eat dinner around 9:00 and stay out and about until 2:00 or so in the morning. I've not experienced that on this trip. But I know it's happening; I can hear it.

As I lay in bed, sleepless, I realize my feet hurt worse than any day yet on the trail. I think that trying to keep up with the gang this afternoon has really taken a toll. I pushed harder than I should have. I am a slow walker, and I best accept that. The slow pilgrim.

Meanwhile, my mind wanders. I begin to worry that the Camino will end before I get my answers, before I can even figure out my questions.

Day 12: July 20
Azofra – Santo Domingo, 9 miles

I'm on the road by 7:00 a.m. to start today's nine-mile excursion. Mid-morning I pause on the outskirts of the next town.

"*Buen camino*," call out a couple of young men who have set up a stand underneath a tree, surrounded by a few benches and picnic tables. They're selling cold drinks and

On the road again.

fresh fruit -- so very appropriate for the weather. I buy a slice of watermelon and take a seat, take my shoes off, and rest for about 20 minutes.

My next stop is for a *café con leche* in Cirueña – a bit of a ghost town, home to a fancy golf course in the middle of nowhere. Some people live there and the club house on the golf course is open, but its glory days were never seen. Spain passed through a housing bubble during its development and it never became the community hoped for. The club house and its coffee are unimpressive. The best part of stopping is a moment's reprieve from the sun. I still have 3.5 miles to go.

I reach Santo Domingo late morning and leave the dirt roads to now navigate the hot cement of bustling city sidewalks. I see a sandwich board sign announcing hamburger plate specials at a restaurant just ahead. That sounds great and I'm hungry. How wonderful to find a good old fashioned hamburger, French fries and coke! I place my order and sit at a shaded table outside.

Almost there, I think to myself as I free my feet from my hiking boots. I take off my socks and wiggle my toes. It feels so good.

I'm excited to see the waitress bringing my plate. I thank her and turn to dig in. I'm surprised to discover that the patty in my *ham*burger really is ham. A thick ham steak! So disappointing, but I eat it. Most of it.

I check into my hostel just past noon. This *albergue* is a cold, old, stone convent built for nuns. Interesting. A nun shows me to my room, to the kitchen area and to an open grassy courtyard in the back where I can do laundry. The other side of the courtyard is a large, more modern building where the nuns live these days.

I wash my clothes and hang them in the sun to dry. Passing through the kitchen I get an idea – ice! I find the nun and ask if I can get some ice to soothe my aching heels. Of course! She's most helpful as I follow her back to the kitchen. She gives me a plastic baggie and fills it with ice. I find a table in a shaded area in the courtyard, elevate my feet, and rest my heels on the ice while I sit and write in my journal. It's heavenly. An occasional light breeze makes me smile, and I'm thankful.

I hobble into town and sit alone at an outside café. It's in the middle of a lot of foot traffic, a good place to watch the night life. There seems to be some sort of festival starting up. Again, I'm reminded of how that Spain comes alive in the evening and families fill the streets. There's music and laughter, . . . all of which I have to leave to get back to my room by 10:00 p.m. when they'll lock the doors.

Back in the convent I find I'm rooming with a young woman from the Czech Republic. She's also traveling alone. We chat a short while before we turn out the lights, close our eyes, and leave our bodies to be eaten by mosquitos. I unfortunately had unloaded the mosquito spray I had purchased a few days prior. I thought I didn't need it any longer, so I dropped it off in a donation box at another hostel to lighten my backpack. Oh well, I'll survive.

CHAPTER 5

Keep walking and your heart will catch up.

Day 13: July 21
Santo Domingo – Grañon, 4 miles

Wonderful, cool cloud cover follows my short four-mile walk to Grañon today. It's lovely walking in the cool air and I'm not so grumpy. I'm not even complaining. I would have continued much further if it hadn't been for the need to rest my heels. Not only that, but Debbie had told me about an unusual and special hostel in Grañon – inside the 14th century church and monastery San Juan Bautista. I want to stay here.

When I arrive, Laura greets me. She's a volunteer giving two weeks to serve as one of the two hosts for us pilgrims. She invites me to take a seat while she gives an overview of the hostel.

"There's no charge to stay here," she tells me as I prepare to give her my euros for a bed. She stops me and shares that they accept donations as we leave. They encourage us to give whatever we are moved to give after we've stayed there. In essence, we stay free of charge and we give so that tomorrow's pilgrims will have their needs cared for at no cost as well. It's a *pass it forward* sort of deal, I surmise.

Laura is kind and soft spoken. She tells me that this place is not just about the physical, but also the heart. The heart? My heart is moved as I continue to listen. Laura talks about love and community, looking out for one another.

"Here we will cook together, eat a communal meal, and sing and have a time of sharing after dinner."

Of course, I tear up. It embarrasses me to cry again but I do. I can feel my hurt and broken heart reaching out, responding to the love and care in her voice.

She shows me to the loft upstairs and I'm the first to stake out my bed for the night. Thin pads are lined up very close together on the hard floor. I pick a spot at the end by the wall where there is no one next to me. By the time everyone checks in, the room is a colorful display of sleeping bag liners laid out over the pads.

In the late afternoon several of the young people are sitting in the common area and taking advantage of the guitar sitting against the wall. One after another, they take turns playing and singing,

Sleeping pads line up very close to each other.

sometimes alone and sometimes with the whole group joining in. As others arrive to help prepare dinner, they continue. I wish I had the courage to pick up the guitar and share a few songs myself, but I don't. For some reason I feel paralyzed, stuck. I just can't quite put myself out there. I sit uncomfortably alone.

My fellow pilgrims are mostly college age and have already formed into small cliques on the trail. We prepare the meal together as Laura assigns responsibilities and everyone pitches in. We sit at long tables and eat the fish someone had donated to the hostel. Then we clean up together. But me? I still can't find my place, I feel unconnected . . . even in a place that's set up to create relationships and community. I feel alone and lost until we gather in the choir loft after dinner and Laura asks each of us to share what the Camino is to us.

Several share that they are at a crossroads in life, just finishing college and looking for direction. Some are looking for adventure and a hiking challenge. One is working through sorrow – the loss of her mother.

Me? I share my story.

I'm on the Camino because my husband died and now I'm trying to figure out what's next for me. I was single for 30 years; Phase 1. Phase 2 was 33 years of married life. I'm now widowed and looking for what Phase 3 will be—my next 30 years. The Camino is my transition into widowhood. It's a pilgrimage for me.

It's been hard. My body hurts. Achilles pain makes it hard to walk. I feel alone and lost. I keep asking why am I doing this? Can't I just check in for a week or two at a luxury hotel and sort out phase 3? Why do I need to walk this damn Camino?

And I answer my own question. There is something mystical, magical about the Camino. I'm finding something powerful in this physical-emotional-mental connection I'm experiencing. The hardship of the physical walking seems to open me to grasp more profoundly what I need to hear. It breaks me down. It peels away the layers of stories and lines that I created to get through life with the least resistance. It drills down into my inner essence. On the Camino what I need carves itself into me instead of just laying its truth on my surface in mental assent, without life. I'm seeing a profound

*connection between the body, the mind and
the heart. I'm finding a deep shaking as they
join forces and get on the same page.*

The group listened, really listened. Their responding love and compassion was not spoken, but I could feel it.

Day 14: July 22
Grañon – Belorado, 9.5 miles

This morning I feel like a part of the group. It feels like I belong. I see that being vulnerable as I was last night is a doorway to being accepted. It's an entry into belonging I realize as I walk to the edge of town with some of the group. I give them hugs and *buen camino* wishes as they head on down the road, moving faster than me.

As I follow behind, I breathe in the morning silence and admire the golden wheat fields that flow on both sides of me, bending ever so gently with a light, almost imperceptible breeze. The same breeze touches my soul, inspiring me to reflect on what has changed from last night to this morning.

I've been a shy person all my life. I could never think of anything to contribute to most conversations, and so I was very quiet. In my senior year of high school I became good friends with someone who told me that in previous years she thought I was stuck-up, conceited. But once she got to know me she knew that wasn't so.

Yes, shyness translates as conceitedness. I get it. I had overcome that to a large degree and learned to be more outgoing, learned to push myself beyond what was comfortable. But somehow here on the Camino I've fallen back into shyness in large groups. One-on-one or with just a

Leaving Grañon, feeling connected

few people I'm good. But when there's a large group, and especially when they've already bonded and are a tight family, I lose my voice. My mind goes blank, and I am quiet.

Okay, I realize, I need to own it. I may be coming across as being stuck-up. That's not my intent, but that's likely the vibe I put out and therefore that is the perception of me. I am responsible for that perception and responsible to change it. I determine that I will.

I plan to travel only a short distance again this day, but the little towns I'm passing through have nothing to offer. There's no reason to stop for the night in any of them.

At noon, in 80-degree heat, I'm about to give up. I sit on a bench in a town center to head off a new blister that wants to form on my toe. Paco from Madrid joins me in the shade. He's having trouble with a knee that had been injured years earlier. He's decided to walk only as far as Burgos and then take the bus home to Madrid. He won't finish the Camino as planned this year.

We leave our shaded perch and walk together for a short while until Paco apologizes and says he has to move faster. I understand. It's hard for most people to walk my slow pace. I encourage him to go on, and to take care of his knee. When I reach the next town four miles down the road, I run into him again. He's just getting ready to leave. I'm thinking about checking into a hostel there and ending the day. Paco insists that I rest there, as he had done, and then walk a final three miles to Belorado. It's a larger town that will have more to offer.

"*Buen camino,*" he says, and gets back on the road.

I sit a while and consider calling the number for a taxi. It's posted on a sign near the bench where I sit. I don't. Soon a man and his daughter drive by in a truck and hand me a bottle of cold water. Must be just what I need because it revives me.

I drag myself to Belorado and take a lovely room with its own bathroom at Casa Maslala. A splurge at 25 euros, but worth it. Paul and his wife rent out three rooms in their house as an oasis for pilgrims – tired ones like me. Paul gets me a cloth wrapped around ice to put on my heels as I go to my room to rest, and he invites me to help myself to the ice in the freezer.

When I can finally handle walking again, I go to the town square – a nice, clean large one. It's surrounded by several stores and businesses and restaurants. I sit outside a restaurant, drinking a soda, and here comes John and Vicki, the couple from Ireland who I'd met in Los Arcos. I'm thrilled. They join me for a drink and John recommends the lemon beer, but I already have my coke. Maybe another time.

Later I join them and a few others for dinner. It's so nice, a welcome change from the loneliness I felt at last night's dinner. This type of sharing is such a large part of the charm of the Camino. Hearing that I still have foot pain, John says I should just skip the rest of the Camino and take a bus to the end – beyond Santiago – to Finesterre. That's on the coast and it has beautiful hotels with great views. I give it some serious thought. It's tempting, but I'm not quite ready to quit.

I reaffirm that once again when I return to my room and read more from my book. No, I'm not ready to quit. Me and Much Afraid have a lot to learn on this struggle out of the

Valley of Fear up to the High Places of Joy. Every hardship she overcomes gives me courage in my own journey. I fall asleep knowing it will end well for both of us.

Day 15: July 23
Belorado for extra rest day

Ah, my comfy private room is so nice. The bed is way better than a liner on a thin mat on the floor! I open the window and a cool breeze brushes across my bed. My big blister has healed. Its fluids did indeed re-absorb into my body. I feel good, so I make arrangements with Paul to stay a second night. Today won't be about walking and struggling. Today I will be quiet. Inspired. Today I will meditate and reflect on my journey.

I go to the town square for my morning coffee and sit at an outside table to write in my journal. There are only a few other people around. The town square is mostly empty at this hour. I'm hopeful to get some answers, some clue as to why I'm on Camino. I sit in silence, almost afraid to ask. Afraid to know.

Tears well up, and I fight them back, insisting that I can't sit and cry in a public place. I push through, thinking that I need to learn the language of tears, their innuendos, subtleties and inflections. What are they trying to tell me?

I'm reminded of a poem I wrote while in meditation one morning several months ago. The words had just come pouring out of me.

Slowly They Appear
Slowly they appear,
One by one,
Without invitation, without announcement.
They simply make themselves known as they
Slowly, effortlessly glide over my
cheekbone.

What is it that started this migration?
I don't know.
I only know that I opened my eyelids,
And down they came,
Seeping out from under moist lashes,
Sliding down, only to be wiped away
Or left untouched to dry alone.

Do I acknowledge them? Do I question
them?
I don't. I let them be.
They will tell themselves to me
When they find the words,
When nameless thoughts shift into form,
And blurred expression into clarity.

For now, they simply appear, one by one,
Without understanding, without expectation,
Without asking anything of me except that I
let them be.

As I sit at the shaded table I'm touched by the morning calm, and the word *penance* comes to mind. In fact, it's crossed my mind a few times on the walk. Certainly no one would do this except as penance, as a type of punishment. I look in my online dictionary for its definition -- *a voluntary, self-inflicted expression of repentance.* Putting that together with what I had received about *absolution* on my first day back in Roncesvalles, I start to get some clarity.

This Camino brings together a physical struggle to match the inner breaking of the heart and of the soul. I think that it gives depth and tangibility to what's felt inside. The physical challenge is drawing emotional pain to my conscious mind—to become aware of it, to see it and name it, to absolve it. And there it is—*absolution.*

Too often we try to just handle everything in the mind. Detached. Untouched. Uninvolved. But the power of transformation comes when the flow of life and pain seep through the cracks, when the physical touches the soul. Those emotions express in the physical and present themselves to the mind. The mind is the observer taking it all in . . . and beginning to understand.

Ah, I think. That's the Camino.

It's the beginning of understanding. It's letting go and accepting. It's an unfolding . . . of healing . . . of truth . . . of community.

I have a growing sense of this, and I know it will become clearer as I continue on. I imagine it will still be unfolding long after I've returned home.

Day 16: July 24
Belorado – Burgos (via bus)

Pity. Self-pity. This morning I wake up to a visit from self-pity. Just like the visitor Much Afraid gets in *Hinds' Feet*. It so amazes me how that my Camino walk parallels hers. It's becoming quite apparent that it's no coincidence I decided to read this book again, now, as I make this journey. As Much Afraid did, I also quickly send Self-Pity on her way.

I have a wonderful life and great opportunities. What do I have to feel sorry for – the pain? The fear? Being alone? Sure those feelings pass over me, and that's the point. They *pass over*, but don't lodge in me. I'm not feeding them. I'll keep moving forward. I'm reminded of something I had written to a friend a few days earlier. It moves me now:

"Keep walking step by step," I had advised. "Keep walking and your heart will catch up."

Today for me that means not walking, but getting on a bus to Burgos. Yesterday, I sat at the kitchen table with Paul, my host, to look at a map of the Camino and determine which stops I should bus over. I don't have enough time left to walk the full trail. I can either just keep walking, go as far as I can, then take the bus from there to get to my flight home. Or, I can bus over some of the middle sections and start walking again from Sarria to earn my Compostela, the Camino certificate. I choose the latter.

Given my timetable, we decide I should take the bus from Belorado to Burgos, then from there to Astorga. The bus to Burgos arrives after the bus to Astorga leaves, so I'll need to stay the night in Burgos. That's 284 km/176 miles that I will miss walking. Sadly, that includes the portion of the Camino called the *Meseta* (the plateau). I've read in guidebooks that some pilgrims consider the *Meseta* boring, repetitive and bleak. It can be blistering hot in the summer and has long sections with no trees to provide shade. Books always caution pilgrims to take a lot of water because there are fewer towns and posts along the way.

I was looking forward to the *Meseta* and am sorry to not experience it. It is great for reflection and contemplation. After all, there's nothing around to distract you from your own inner being. Someone had suggested to me that the Camino is divided into three parts. The first portion is physical. That's the section I've been in so far. The second is mental. That's the Meseta where you are totally left to just thinking. The third is spiritual. I believe I've had all of these intertwined along the way so far, but it probably is more pronounced during each section.

Anyway, I'm sure this is the best decision, given my circumstances. In addition to its normal hardship, the region has been experiencing a heat wave this summer. I've heard stories of sunstroke and sickness among those on the *Meseta*. John, the bicyclist who I met in Lorca, plans to cross it at night to avoid the heat. He has studied when there will be a full moon and is setting his schedule accordingly. Me? I'll bus over it.

I rise early, grab coffee and bread in the town plaza, and walk to the bus stop. By the time I get there, I feel good again. Heel pain is gone. I sit on the bus and think more about the work of this Camino. Its job is to break you down so that you can begin anew, or change course. You have to let go of what and where you are to be able to move to something new.

I'm reminded of a greeting card from years ago: "The hardest part is letting go." This is the caption for a trapeze artist in mid-air, letting go of his bar to reach out to be caught by his partner who's swinging toward him. I love that example. We must let go of the old before we can touch the new. Seems to me that this is often necessary before we even have an idea about what the new is! It's a risk. Maybe there is nothing new . . . Maybe I'll reach out and nothing will catch me. Then what? I figure that is today's lesson for me. Let go. Reach out. Trust God.

I think about it more, recalling what Franciscan priest Richard Rohr has written about this phenomenon:

> ". . . reality itself teaches us: painful life situations have to dismantle us brick by brick, decade by decade.

> "Jesus knew that he needed to destabilize a person's false, separate self before they could understand that they had a True Self, but destabilizing our security systems and our ego is always a hard sell. He says, "What does it profit a person if they gain the whole world and lose their soul?" (Luke 9:25)

". . . As God said in the inaugural vision to Jeremiah: "Your job is to take apart and demolish, and then start over building and planting anew" (Jeremiah 1:10)."

Yes, tear down to build up. I do believe this is the purpose of the Camino for me – *to take apart and demolish*, so I can *build and plant something new* that will take me on my next thirty years. This is my journey.

It's still morning when I reach Burgos. I check in to the hostel which is situated over the bus station. Very convenient. Then I become a tourist. It's kind of forced on me because I can't get a bus out to Astorga (my next destination), until tomorrow morning. I have a full day in a huge, bustling, historic city.

I leave my backpack at the hostel and walk just a short distance to tour the Cathedral de Burgos. It's a UNESCO World Heritage site, and rightly so. It contains quite a few distinct chapel s inside and many historic pieces of art and architecture. It's beautiful. Astounding. And a welcome change from my daily grind.

When I exit the cathedral, I do what any girl would do in a big city. I go shopping. There are a number of clothing stores in the immediate area, as well as souvenir shops. My only purchases are flip flop sandals and socks. I wouldn't dare add any more weight than that to my backpack. The socks are light weight and a good change from the heavy woolen ones I've been wearing. The flip flops are to wear in my down time around the hostel. But after I buy them, I start to realize that it is the wearing flats that makes my heels hurt so badly. When I'm in my hiking shoes, I feel better. Those shoes have heels plus inserts which I've added in the heels.

It's a long but easy-going day and it ends with a special treat. Near sundown, I go out once again to escape the heat of my room with eight bunk beds that are now filling in. I hear chamber music nearby and follow the sound to a free concert in the courtyard of a small museum. It's full. Standing room only. I edge my way toward a column where there's a small space left to lean against. A soprano is singing an aria, accompanied by a string quartet. Next, the soprano is replaced by a flautist. I play flute myself, so this is very special. I'm in heaven, especially when an occasional breeze waltzes through.

I'm very happy, very thankful, very grateful for such a nice and unexpected surprise.

Day 17: July 25
Burgos – Santa Catalina, 6 miles (plus bus)

After a miserable night's sleep stuffed in a humid and hot room, I'm up at 5:00 a.m. to catch my 6:00 bus. That's easy. The hostel is right over the bus station. The hard part is finding a someone to unlock the door to let me out since they don't unlock it until 6:00. I find someone in the kitchen preparing breakfast service. All is well.

I arrive in Astorga four hours later. What a lovely town! I pass by the Episcopal Palace of Astorga, designed by Spanish architect Antonio Gaudi whose work I adore. His use of light is brilliant, as seen in this building. I regret that I can't spend time here to explore more of his works.

I have breakfast at an outdoor café and then hit the road. I'll cover only six miles by foot today, getting as far as

The Episcopal Palace of Astorga is a neo-Gothic style building designed by Gaudi. But he didn't finish it. For some reason he quit and burned the plans. It was later finished by Ricardo Garcia Guereta in 1915.

Santa Catalina. Quickly, the heat makes me weary and my body is starting to give me new concern.

My left knee feels like it wants to twist or pop. It had, in fact, done that just three years ago. On the day of my husband's memorial service, it popped and swelled and I couldn't walk on it for a week. It has been given to weakness off and on since then. To be extra careful, I decide that after today I'll send my backpack ahead by taxi most days.

I stay the night in Santa Catalina. This hamlet once housed a hospital for pilgrims. Now its population totals only 50. The host at my hostel tells me he lives in a nearby town. We sit on the shaded patio and talk about life – his, mine, and life in general. He traveled the Camino over 30 years ago -- on horseback. That is rare these days, he tells me, but back then it was common. He's still in contact with some of the people he rode with on that trip, mainly through annual Christmas cards. It's interesting how such relationships continue for years.

Later, when his shift is up and he's going home, he finds me to say good-bye. He says he enjoyed talking with me, that I'm an interesting woman, and he asks if he can give me a kiss on the cheek.

"*Sí,*" I tell him and accept his peck on the cheek, like the Spaniards do. I enjoyed talking with him. He has no idea how meaningful our little conversation was to me. I appreciate his kindness and care.

Such kindness and care are a constant at this stop. My roommates tonight include John and Mark, brothers who are both doctors from Seattle, Washington. They are travelling with their three teenage sons, walking the Camino in sections – two weeks at a time. This is their third trip over the past few years. They started in Burgos this year. I've met several pilgrims who do the Camino in stages when their schedule doesn't afford them a full month or more off. It's very practical and certainly makes it more accessible.

We talk throughout the afternoon and I enjoy watching their close family dynamic. And the energy! While I put my feet up and rest, the three teens take off to race each other down the street. *Oh to be young!* I appreciate that they are having this great experience while they're still so young and that they're having it with their fathers. It's refreshing.

As Mark and I talk, I share my story of being a widow. He asks if I ever get lonely walking alone.

"Yes, I do," I answer. "A lot."

My truthfulness surprises me. I normally would try to hide that pain and put a soft spin on it, as if I feel it's a flaw in my character. But it isn't a flaw, and I'm learning to be more honest. Mark tells me about a widow they met in a previous year, a 30-something year old woman. Hiking the Camino had been her husband's dream. He died, and she was on the Camino to scatter his ashes along the way.

He invites me to join him and his family for dinner in the hostel's restaurant later. I happily accept.

Next I meet George from France. He heard me comment on the pain in my heels and says he can help me with it. "That would be great," I tell him. He asks me to put my foot up on his lap, and he begins to press on key pressure points up and down the calf. He rubs the foot and turns it side to side.

Just as George is finishing the first foot, Mark steps up and tells me they're heading in for dinner now. I have the sense that he's actually checking to make sure that George is not taking advantage of me. Sweet. They talk a bit and we learn George has worked alongside medics somewhere, somehow. Language is a barrier and I don't fully understand just what he does or where he learned how to do it. Meanwhile, Mark heads indoors and I tell him I'll be there soon. George begins the other foot.

I think George is a miracle worker. The pain completely leaves and I would love to sit with him much longer, but I have a dinner engagement I'm looking forward to. I thank George. As I walk away I feel better than I have in months.

I do enjoy the dinner company. We share stories. We laugh and I'm encouraged. Once again, life is good.

CHAPTER 6

I didn't even cry.

Day 18: July 26
Santa Catalina – Rabanal, 8 miles

In the middle of my eight miles today, I note that I've now personally walked 100 miles across Spain. I feel pride. It's a good achievement.

That awareness helps to offset the misery I feel with the very hard, bitter cold wind blowing through me. It's tough going today, but I then judge it to be better than the unforgiving summer heat that's been dogging me most days.

I arrive at a lovely hostel in Rabanal, its courtyard lined by flowers, vibrant green trees and a festive line of colorful chairs. I contemplate just picking up my backpack (which is here waiting for me) and to keep walking. However, after some internal debate, I defer to my knee's whispering plea. She's asking me to take it easy and rest. She doesn't hurt, but she's on the brink.

I pay extra for a private room, rather than share the dormitory setting with fellow pilgrims. It's a very small room upstairs. Just enough space to tuck one twin bed and a small night stand in between narrow walls. I appreciate that it has a window which I immediately open for fresh, cool air. I rationalize the room is worth the extra cost because I will likely be crying tonight in anticipation of tomorrow. That's when I'll place a stone at the *Cruz de Ferro* (Iron Cross) as a final farewell to David my love, my life partner, my companion for 33 years. Yes, I'll need some privacy.

Soon, what threatened to be a difficult day emotionally, turns into one of great joy. I'm sitting downstairs in the restaurant, eating my rice with vegetables, and in walks Amy.

Amy! My South Korean friend from the beginning of the walk. I hadn't seen her since she had pulled ahead of me that first day two and a half weeks ago.

We both scream and hug. It's so exciting! We spend the afternoon catching up on our travels, our aches and pains and blisters, and what sections of the Camino we bused across and where we walked. It's fabulous. We make plans to head out together in the morning. We'll visit the *Cruz* (the cross) together.

In the evening I go to vespers at the town's Catholic church. It's the first time I've ever been in such a service. It's lovely and calming. It's conducted in Latin, but a translation of the service is printed in several languages, including English. I follow along and feel comforted.

Turns out I don't even cry tonight.

Day 19: July 27
Rabanal – El Acebo, 6 miles

It rained all night, but has stopped long enough for Amy and me to get a good start on the road without getting wet. We talk and laugh. Amy tries to teach me how to pose for pictures. She's really good at it, a natural model, very photogenic. I try but just look silly. I'm missing something and feel too self-conscious. But it's fun and entertaining as we walk.

We quickly get to the next village, a small enclave of just a few buildings really, and we stop for breakfast. Amy has a bowl of cereal; it's the only time I've seen cereal on the Camino. It looks so good! I regret I didn't order a bowl rather than my fried eggs. Still, my eggs are a good break from the standard croissant with coffee and orange juice.

Cathay and Amy, reunited in Rabanal

Once we gear up again and head out, it's starting to rain lightly. It mists and sprinkles off and on during the final mile to the *Cruz*. I don't mind. The mist surrounding us seems appropriate for the task at hand.

The *Cruz de Ferro* (Iron Cross) is at one of the highest elevations of the Camino. At its peak, there is a tall wooden pole topped by an iron cross. For centuries, even before it was a Camino landmark, it was a Celtic place of ritual. These days, pilgrims typically bring a stone from home to leave there. For many it represents letting go a burden.

When my friends Peter and David did the Camino three years ago, they each carried a rock from my husband's fish aquarium to leave at the cross in his remembrance. Peter later shared with me that it had been a very emotional experience. Other pilgrims stopped and joined with them to honor David, listening to stories about him and how he touched lives. He told me that everyone was crying and laughing. Crying and laughing. Such an appropriate memorial for my David.

Now I'm standing in that same place. The air is damp and cold. Mist and sullen clouds fill the sky. Any sunshine that tries to peak out doesn't have a chance. I like that. I don't want sunshine. Not here. I want to feel the heaviness of this moment. And I do.

My first task is to let go of two pebbles I've carried from home. They represent two young women, daughters of my good friend, who are struggling to find their way in life. I've prayed for the two of them each day on the Camino. In my heart they are filling in for several young people I know who also struggle.

As the pebbles fall from my hand, they move briskly, bouncing from one rock to another until they finally lay still in a place of their own. I see the symbolism in this. I close my eyes and pray that the two women, and all the young people they represent, will do the same. Maybe they're being tossed about in life right now, but may they find their place and settle in where they belong.

Next I reach into my pocket and take out the small stone I picked up at *Alto de Perdón* the day I forgave David for dying and leaving me. I slowly reach down to the pile of rocks at my feet. Small ones, large ones, round, flat. Some have phrases written on them. Others have names and dates. Some, like mine, are plain. Their mere presence is a message and is sufficient. I find just the right landing and set it down, nestled among a collection of similar stones. David would approve, I'm sure. I touch it with my fingers, running them across its smooth surface, and I whisper my final good-bye.

Pilgrims from around the world lay stones at the Cruz de Ferro/Iron Cross.

Amy hugs me and we cry together. I'm so glad to not be alone.

We turn our attention back to the road. I had read in the travel guides that the descent from the *Cruz* is a very steep and difficult passage. When wet, it can be slippery and dangerous, so Amy and I opt to take a taxi to our next stop – a new hotel / hostel in El Acebo. Amy is excited because it has a swimming pool . . . even though this is hardly swimming weather.

We get to the hotel and check in to a nice room with four sets of bunk beds. We each stake out a bottom bed. Despite that it's cold and the sun is nowhere to be found, I let Amy talk me into taking a swim with her in the pool. Not surprisingly, we're the only ones here. That's good because I'm slightly embarrassed in my swimsuit. It's actually black panties and sports bra – which do look like a simple two-piece swimsuit. I had read this suggestion in a guide book in preparation for the trip. You certainly don't want the extra weight of carrying a swim suit you'll only use a few times. And I must say, it's a good idea. It covers more than most two-piece swimsuits cover.

Occasionally someone comes by, looks at us as if we're crazy and asks if the water is cold. "Yes, it is" we tell them, and they leave. We manage to hang out poolside almost an hour, but finally decide it's time to get inside and warm up.

We find two women from Germany have checked in and will be rooming with us. We visit for a while, then they rest. I splurge and pay for a massage I read about at check-in. Nice. My heels stop hurting, probably because of the intense workout on the calves.

Amy, the two from Germany, and I enjoy a nice dinner and conversation in the restaurant, then return to our room. I know I'll sleep well tonight. The room is cool, quiet, and I feel revived and rested.

Day 20: July 28
El Acebo – Ponferrada, 10 miles

I woke up rested and feeling good, and I soon realize how much I needed that because the walk is not any easier today. Amy quickly moves on ahead of me and says that she will wait for me in the first bar in the next town.

The descent from El Acebo is the scariest, the most difficult I've ever encountered. It's very steep, over loose stone in some places . . . you just never know which stones will be firm and which will slide on you. Every muscle in my body is being called into play. I laugh at the thought of *Hinds' Feet on High Places*. I could certainly use those sure-footed hinds' feet now. If I could turn around and go back up to the start to grab a taxi, I would. However, trying to go back up would be even more difficult than continuing downward. I'm afraid, but deep inside know I can do it. After all, I have to. There really is no choice.

(It was only later I learned more than one pilgrim has fallen on these rocks and arrived a bloody mess at the next town. That's why, as I also later learned, there is an alternate – and highly recommended – route which runs alongside the highway. What I had used is what may have once been an old Roman road, but it's fallen into decay and is now *almost* impassible at points.)

Once I'm back on firm and level ground, I decide I can do anything. Absolutely anything. There is nothing that I cannot do. Yep, I've got hinds' feet for sure. I am unstoppable.

It's taken me so long to get down through the El Acebo pass that I figure Amy has surely given up on me and moved on ahead. I get to the next town, cross a stone bridge and step into the first bar I see. It's pretty crowded. I don't see her, but I'm hungry so I put in an order for eggs, bacon and toast. That's a treat and I deserve it, I think to myself. Outside on the patio I see a man who was also dining at the same hotel Amy and I were in last night. He invites me to join him.

I share with John that I was going to meet up with my friend here but I don't see her. "The young lady you were eating with last night?" he asks. "She's right over there," he says pointing to a table of young women off to the side.

Amy was sitting with her back to us. She heard his comment and came over. I don't know how I missed her but I was glad she was there. She didn't find the mountain descent as traumatic as I did. Of course, she's a lot younger and more sure-footed than I am. Plus, I suspect *impossible* and *dangerous* don't register in her vocabulary. We visit while I eat, then arrange to meet again in Ponferrada. Amy gives me the name of the hostel she's picked. She'll check in and save a bed for me.

Ponferrada, with a population of 69,000, is interesting. I find Amy and we go out to look for something to eat. It's Sunday afternoon and we're having trouble finding a restaurant. We finally end up in a restaurant / convenience store at a big gas stop at the edge of the highway. The restaurant has a limited menu and we decide to share a pizza. We take a seat at one of the tables and look around. We see mostly men. Seated in groups of 3 – 5. Many of them are playing checkers or chess. It's apparent this is a Sunday afternoon tradition for the menfolk of the city. I wonder where the women are.

Leaving there, we pass back by our hostel and go to the other side to see what's there. The main city is there! There are a lot of restaurants and a multitude of people walking around the plaza. It's a whole different scene, and that's where the women, and couples, and families are wandering about on this hot Sunday afternoon. That's also where a huge castle is located.

I tour the Castle of the Knights Templar and learn about its history. The Order of the Knights Templar was active for a couple of centuries during the Middle Ages. It was a military order endorsed by the Catholic Church. They were pledged to guard Christians on pilgrimages everywhere. In 1178 it set up headquarters in this castle to protect pilgrims on their way to Santiago.

It seems the Knights Templar gained a lot of popularity and power; and just as importantly, a lot of financial wealth. So much so that religious and political leaders looked for ways to bring them down and finally did so through King Phillip IV of France. Long story short, the leaders succeeded with a smear campaign and the Pope officially ordered the Knights Templar to disband in 1312.

Today the castle houses the Templars' Library and the Ponferrada Investigation and Study Centre. I read that its collection includes almost 1400 books, including facsimile editions of works by Leonardo da Vinci. It's a most interesting place.

Day 21: July 29
Ponferrada – Cacabelos, 9 miles

Amy and I start out the day together, navigating our way out of the big city. The markers are not easy to follow. Half the time I question if we're headed in the right direction, but Amy plows ahead without doubt. And she leads us well. Once outside of the city we again separate as she pulls ahead in her fast pace. She's eager to get to Santiago with enough time to travel on to Finesterre on the coast before catching a bus to Portugal. From there she'll travel a few more weeks in Europe before returning to South Korea.

By the time I reach Cacabelos, I've been scratching my body incessantly. Bed bugs. I just know it. When I checked in yesterday, the bed assigned to me in Amy's room was an upper bunk. Given my heel issues I didn't want to try going up and down to get in it so I asked for a lower bunk. They gave me one in another room.

While I was resting, a couple of Chinese women came in. They looked over their beds next to mine and through broken English and pantomime told me they're leaving – that the bed has bed bugs. I thought they were over reacting, but I did get up and examine my bed closely, hoping I actually knew what to look for. I didn't see anything so I stayed.

Last night the room was so very hot and humid, an often repeated pattern on this Camino in July. I crawled out from my silk liner and laid directly on the mattress and evidently unknowingly exposed myself to the ugly little critters. The women were right. I wish I had left and gone to another room with them.

Reaching my stop in Cacabelos I tell the host that I think I have bed bugs. She quickly takes a look at the bites on my stomach and dismisses them. No, I'm fine, she says and she assigns me my room. I shower and see the bites lined up three in a row on my stomach, and another set deepening on my back. They are bed bugs.

I spend the afternoon at a laundromat. The attendant helps me to wash everything in very hot water. A specific poison is recommended to kill bed bugs, but the pharmacy doesn't have it in stock. They recommend another product in hopes it will help. When I get back to my hostel I convince the host that these are bed bug bites. We spray my backpack and put it in a black trash bag and stuff it in a dark storage room. I've read it needs to be in the heat, in the sun, but there is no outside space here to do that. So I cross my fingers.

Exhausted, frustrated, and sad, I lay on my bed. Through all I've endured – the ups and downs and all the pains – these bed bugs are the worst. I think maybe I should just pack up and go home. I've done well to hold on this long, but enough is enough. Maybe I will take a bus on over to Finesterre and take a few weeks in vacation mode.

Then Patrick, a solo traveler from the UK, comes in and sets his bedroll on the bunk above me. "How's your day going?" he asks.

"I've got bed bugs," I tell him. "I've spent the afternoon at the laundromat trying to get rid of them. I feel like giving up and going home," and I begin to cry.

Standing in front of my bed Patrick sweetly reaches out his hand and asks if he can hold my hand. "Yes," I say.

He lowers himself to the floor and sits cross-legged next to me, taking my hand. "Bed bugs are just a part of the Camino experience," he says. He continues talking about life and its ups and downs. I don't really remember just what else he said, I only know that he's comforting and I stop crying.

I settle down and join Patrick for a walk around town. Our talk takes my mind off my woes. He has a gentle spirit and keen wisdom. I think he could easily be a counselor or therapist by trade, but I learn he's a mechanical engineer. That becomes apparent also as he describes the structure of the Roman bridge we are looking at. He's quite detailed and he's quite studied in the history of the area.

As we continue to walk we share about our lives and hopes. Then he stops, turns to me, and with one sentence he unravels my Camino mystery. "You're here to learn to fall in love with yourself again," he says.

My soul immediately shifts into this knowing and confirms to me that this is my journey. This is why I'm here.

We stop for dinner before returning to the room. Patrick's interesting company and I learn about him serving alongside a Canadian brigade during Desert Storm and how he grew to appreciate their integrity and ingenuity. I'm quite fascinated with his life experiences. Now in his 50s he's at a fork in the road, embarking on a new career path when he leaves the Camino. Everyone has something to learn from the road, I'm sure.

As I lay down to sleep, I'm thankful for Patricks' wisdom and gentle manner. I'm thankful for those insightful words:

You're here to learn to fall in love with yourself.

Reading from my book, I see that Much Afraid is learning about the purpose of her journey as well: ". . . for those who go down into the furnace of Egypt and find there the flower of Acceptance come up changed and with the stamp of royalty upon them."

Day 22: July 30
Cacabelos – Pereje, 10 miles

I join Patrick for a cup of coffee before we part ways. I feel encouraged again, happy to walk today's ten miles. All is well. "*Buen camino*," I say to Patrick as he leaves. In my heart that phrase includes deep gratitude and appreciation.

It's a short 3.5 miles to Villafranca where I decide to stop for breakfast. I meander through the cobblestone streets of the sizeable town with a population of 3500, until I realize

I'm once again at the outskirts still without anything to eat. I pass a young woman with backpack and I ask her if she knows where I can find breakfast. "Yes," she says and tells me that the main center is back behind us, I had passed by on the edges of it.

"Oh," I say, clearly disappointed that I had passed it.

Reading my face, she says, "It's so strange to me that we walk all these miles without thought, but we never want to retrace our steps a short distance back to something we may have missed."

"That's so true!" I laugh. I thank her and turn to go back into the town center, smiling at what strange creatures we are. What's the problem with adding another tenth of a mile to my walk to enjoy a good breakfast? I have to ask directions again a time or two, but when I get to the plaza I not only enjoy a good tortilla española breakfast, but I see they have set up a farmer's market. It's wonderful! I spend an extra hour wandering and looking at the goods, so tempted to buy a dress, some sandals, some knickknacks, anything! But I don't. I resist temptation because I don't want to add any weight to my pack which I'm still carrying with me rather than sending it ahead by taxi most days.

Refreshed and content, I make a mental note of Villafranca as a beautiful place to spend a few days if I should one day return to the Camino. Its medieval and Renaissance character is very picturesque. The name itself, Villafranca, means "city of foreigners." They must be used to people like me walking around.

The beautiful *Puerta de Perdón* (Door of Forgiveness) ushers people into *Iglesia de Santiago* (St. James Church). In ancient times, pilgrims who became sick and were unable to reach Santiago could still receive absolution and completion of their pilgrimage if they made it as far as these doors.

That's not an option for me. I walk back to the bridge where I had stopped previously. There are two paths from here. One is to follow a narrow footpath beside the highway, noisy and with some dangerous bends. The second is a challenging and steep scenic walk uphill and back down. I decide to take my chances on the highway . . . *taking my chances* is right, I find out.

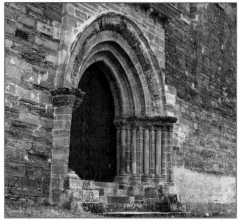

Puerta de Perdón/Door of Forgiveness

I stop in Pereje. I'm the first to check in at the 55-bed municipal *albergue* and I stake out my bed at what I hope to be a cool section of the dorm. Most of the 30 beds in my room get filled throughout the afternoon. I'm happy to be the first to shower – no worry about running out of hot water which can happen if you're a late arriver. Sadly, I see new bites on my body – can it be bed bugs still?

Surely not, I hope.

CHAPTER 7

Good night. Sleep tight. Don't let the bed bugs bite.

Day 23: July 31
Pereje – Vega de Valcarce, 9 miles

The cute bed bug saying my mother used to send me to bed with is no longer endearing. It depicts the nightmare I'm living. Bed bugs are biting. Now not only my back, but my neck as well.

I open an email from Amy and learn she's stopped nine miles up the road at the Albergue El Paso in Vega de

Valcarce. She was running fever and feeling weak, so she's staying an extra day. I tell her about my bed bug problem and she immediately writes back that I should get to El Paso. She says the host is really helpful. I pack and head out. On the way through town I stop at a pharmacy and they sell me the toxic spray that should help kill these little monsters.

I get to El Paso before noon and Amy's right. The host is really helpful.

Getting rid of bed bugs -- All my clothes spread out in the sun

"I've got bed bugs," I say to Lalo, the host. He doesn't even flinch.

We pull everything out of my backpack and spread it all in the sun on the rock wall lining the entry to the hostel. Lalo sprays them with the killer spray. He then puts my backpack in a large black trash bag, sprays it heavily with the poison, and ties it closed. He sets it on a stone ledge in the sun. (And it stays there for three days until I repack it to move on.)

Now the tricky part is to find something to cover my body while *all of my clothing* lay in the sun. As I've mentioned, most hostels have a box for items that pilgrims want to discard, and others can help themselves to anything that interests them. I myself had left a dress at a hostel a week earlier. I brought it to wear in Paris in the days before starting the Camino. I used it a time or two since then, and finally decided to free myself from its weight.

Lalo digs through donations at El Paso and comes back to me with a white shirt that actually fits me. But for my bottom half – all he can find is a large red quick-dry towel. It doesn't completely cover me. I'm embarrassed. So I keep on my gray pants I'd bought in Logroño. I figure I'll just throw them away after today.

Lalo gives me a tour of the place. There are a few rooms of 8 beds, and a private room with two beds. I tell him I think I may want to pay extra for the private one, . . . because "I may need a place to cry this afternoon," I say with a smile.

"No," says Lalo. "If you need to cry . . ." and he pats his shoulder indicating that's where I should do any crying. So sweet. I resist the urge to try it out now.

He shows me to the other rooms, including one where Amy is lying down, recovering from her ailments. Once again, it's so wonderful to see her familiar, jovial face. We laugh and hug, and I'm so thankful she insisted I come here. I take a bed in her room.

Amy and I walk up the street to eat hamburgers. Real ones this time, not the ham kind. They're as good as any I've ever eaten in the USA. Lunch is shared over conversation with three women from Canada. They're travelling together – one to celebrate that she has overcome cancer, one to bully the cancer recently diagnosed in her body, and the third a friend to both of them. They're inspiring. They remind me that I'm not alone. Everyone has a story on the Camino. It gives us an instant bond and appreciation for one another if we slow down enough to take notice and to listen.

By mid-afternoon I'm really tired and need to rest. But I can't lay on my bed because if I do, my pants will transfer bedbugs to the bed. Left with no choice, I strip off my pants, fold the red towel diagonally, and cinch it at my waist. I take my pants outside, spray them and add them to the rest of my wardrobe in the sun. In the end, I suppose the towel covers all it really needs to cover. It just shows more leg than I generally like to show, a sexier look than what I'm used to. Amy and I laugh and she documents my dilemna with a photo.

More leg than I generally like to show

In the evening we join Lalo on the patio and watch a

114

mother bird feed her young in a nest she has built under the awning. So peaceful. So relaxing. Amy and I laugh a lot and inform Lalo that we'll be returning next year to help him run the hostel.

Meanwhile, once the sun goes down Lalo removes my clothes from the rock wall, washes them in the hottest washing machine setting, and then puts them in the dryer. He returns them to me bug free and neatly folded in a basket. Trauma is over. I'm in a wonderful place. An oasis.

Day 24: August 1
Rest Day in Vega de Valcarce

Amy leaves early in the morning. I'm staying another day. We talk about trying to meet up in Santiago if possible. Of course, she'll be there before me. But she's going on to Finesterre and maybe will be back about the time I arrive. I hope I'll see her again.

My feet -- my heels to be exact -- hurt quite a bit. Walking is so painful. I once again contemplate whether to continue or not. After all, 24 days and 150 miles is a big accomplishment. But where will I stay if I don't continue the Camino? And will I be able to live with myself if I stop early? I decide to stay at El Paso one more day and come to a decision tomorrow.

Meanwhile, I had a good rest last night. I go to a nearby café for breakfast. I drink my coffee and eat my toast while watching pilgrims walk down main street, readying their climb up to O'Cebreio. Vega de Valcarce is the last town before going up the mountain. An hour later I walk down a side street and find a shade tree at the edge of the Valcarce River, and stretch out on the grass underneath it. I listen to Jason Mraz on my iPhone and soak in the peace. Not a care in the world. Total relaxation.

Returning to the hostel, I sit my feet in the cool running water flowing by the rock wall. Lalo created this little stream for just this purpose. I think about how many pilgrims have sat here with their feet in this small canal. I'm glad that I'm one of them. In the background Simon and Garfunkel are singing, serenading Lalo as he cleans the rooms in preparation for the next round of travelers. Tears fill my eyes. This time because my soul is comforted. I feel fortunate. At the same time, because I don't know what to do. I don't know where to go when I leave Spain.

Up until now my direction in life had been so clear, so obvious. David was a Christian pastor and evangelist, part of an international board of elders. We worked side by side throughout our 33 years together. I also had worked part-time in the field of adult literacy, but my primary focus was the ministry – ministry and David. We never had children, but we travelled a lot. To some extent, I think doing a lot of travel compensated for not having children to have to stay home and tend to. At least that's the line I would add when people asked if we had children. "No, no children. I guess that's why we're

116

able to travel so much." It was never a choice; it just happened that way.

When David passed, I think I was able to do well because of the strength of our relationship. I knew what I had with him was special and it satisfied me. I was strong as I began to negotiate my way under new circumstances. Those new circumstances were not just that I was widowed, but included leaving the ministry organization I had been a part of all my adult life – the organization I had been a part of even before meeting David. A new awareness and awakening was unfolding within me and I knew I couldn't continue as I had. I felt a strong sense of my purpose calling me elsewhere.

After David passed I continued living a year in Los Angeles, then moved to a farm in Indiana where friends took me in as part of their family. It was a good place for me, a safe place. The slower pace with fewer distractions gave me a chance to recalibrate. To meditate. To consider my life's purpose.

Being on the Camino is a continuation of that journey. I believe it will bring me into some greater clarity of where I belong in my next 30 years. But first, it's bringing me a lot of discord, frustration and pain. I've been fiercely independent the past couple of years and have freely moved about, visiting friends and enjoying life. I've enjoyed the freedom that a single person experiences. But more and more I'm thinking that maybe I don't want to be alone. I'm sure I'll know more by the time I reach Santiago.

Meanwhile, today I feel like I can breathe again, feel again, live again, after being in a long dark tunnel. I feel myself coming alive, becoming settled. I'm aware of the environment, of nature, of life itself, and I feel more of a connection with it.

Lalo stops his chores for a moment and tells me that he'll make lunch for us – *tortilla española* (potato quiche). "Wonderful," I say. "Can I help? I want to learn how to make it." He says I can watch if I like, but the first step is peeling and slicing potatoes and no need to watch that. Tells me I should sit outside and enjoy the air; when it's time for the next step he'll call me.

I take a seat in a red plastic chair at the picnic table on the grass. It's shaded under a wooden pergola. As I'm writing in my journal, Lua appears out of nowhere. Lua is a beautiful black, white and gray Border Collie with the bluest, most penetrating eyes. I learn she's from the neighborhood and visits often. To my surprise, she drops a rock at my feet and looks up at me.

"Are you inviting me to play?" I ask. It seems she is so I get up and we begin to play fetch. We're near the stream and I step into it to cool my feet while we play. Lua steps in also and cools her feet. She picks up another rock to give me and we continue the game. Charming.

"Lua, leave Cathay alone," calls out Lalo. "She has to come and eat now. She'll play with you later." Taking my cue, I go into the kitchen and get my lesson in making *tortilla española*.

We eat at the picnic table in the cool air. The tortilla is accompanied by flavorful ripe tomatoes just picked from Lalo's garden, and a cold beer. As we talk I learn Lalo had lived in Barcelona but came to Vega de Valcarce after an economic downturn ended his career as a textile designer. Four years ago he and his cousin opened this hostel. He's clearly very relaxed and content. Maybe it's contagious because I'm beginning to feel the same.

I continue to sit outside throughout the afternoon. I watch a man sit on a small tractor and mow the large grassy field between the hostel buildings and the Valcarce River. An older man walks behind him, helping to form the cut grass into round bales. It's an impressive operation – and even more so when Lalo tells me that the older man is 91 years old. They later join Lalo for a beer. It's a nice life. I could learn a lot from them.

It was a lovely day. I'm learning how to sit and relax, to enjoy the quiet, to experience peace inside and out. I'm feeling so well taken care of, and spoiled. Especially when I go to bed and realize that I have the big 8-bed room all to myself. Several pilgrims had checked in throughout the day, but Lalo put them in the other rooms, leaving me to my privacy. Sweet.

Day 25: August 2
Another Rest Day in Vega de Valcarce

La reina (the queen) is what Lalo calls me, and rightly so because I feel like a queen. I soak my feet in the stream again before going to town for breakfast. On the way back I notice a hair salon around the corner. *Why not?* I go in and have my roots colored and cut refreshed. It feels wonderful.

Back at the hostel the pilgrims are steadily arriving. We end with a pretty full house. *"We"* I say, as if I'm half owner. It feels that comfortable though.

Lalo invites me for lunch again. He makes pasta with olive oil and tomatoes. Simple and delicious. We're joined at the picnic table by a Spanish couple from the Canary Islands. We're still at the table a few hours later when a camera crew from a local TV station, La 8 Bierzo, comes to talk with us. They're doing a story on the Camino and would like to interview us. "I'm so glad I went to the beauty salon," I joke. "I'm ready for my debut on Spanish television!" We do the interview.

(Months later when I'm back home in the USA Lalo emails and tells me he saw me on television! Sadly, the video never made its way to YouTube so I haven't seen it.)

Lalo tells me that he's sorry, but he won't be able to give me a private suite tonight. A lot of pilgrims have checked in throughout the day and most beds are filled. I room with a mother/daughter team from the Czeck Republic and with Agatha, a solo traveler from Paris. As Agatha and I get ready to go for dinner, Lalo stops us. He's quite charming as he engages us with card tricks – correctly identifying which card we each choose from the deck. I've always been in awe of such; and to tell the truth, frustrated by it. I can't see how he does it, and I get frustrated with what I cannot understand. It seems as though he has mysterious powers, and I'm rather smitten with him.

I'm not very hungry but I appreciate the conversation with Agatha as we have dinner. She's had a remarkable recovery from a severe car accident she had in 2003. She lost language and all vocabulary. Through work with a speech therapist and a neurologist, she recovered over a period of several years. Once again, I'm humbled and inspired by the life experiences of a fellow pilgrim.

In the evening I visit a little with the mother / daughter roommates. They have a lovely system in which they start out together each morning. When the mother has walked as far as she can for the day, she takes a taxi for the remainder and meets her daughter at the next hostel. What a wonderful way for them to travel together. I admire them and the intimate time they are able to share.

My shoes at the door of Albergue El Paso

CHAPTER 8

I am an amazing woman.

Day 26: August 3
Vega de Valcarce – La Faba, 5 miles

E ver so sadly, I pack my bag to leave my oasis, El Paso. I had arrived feeling defeated and depressed. Heel pain was relentless. More than that, the bed bugs had been my last straw. I seriously considered not continuing to walk any further, but simply to hang out somewhere for the remaining couple of weeks until I could catch my flight home. I thought maybe I could just hang out at this hostel for a week or so. But I know it's time to go. I know I'm not done with the Camino . . . or perhaps it's that the Camino isn't done with me.

El Paso has given me the rest and rejuvenation I need. I have watched a bird feed her young, soaked my feet in a stream, listened to beautiful music, played fetch with a neighborhood dog, laid on the grass, been cooked for and entertained. Ah the Camino - up and down and up and down. El Paso was a nice *up*.

On parallel path, Much Afraid found a little golden flower. She then realized it had been transplanted and was actually growing in her own heart, giving her delight. It said to her, "Behold me, here I am, growing in your heart, 'Acceptance-with-Joy'".

With some "Acceptance-with-Joy" in my own heart, I say good-bye to Lalo and turn to start the steep climb to O'Cebreio.

"If you have any trouble, let me know and I'll send a car for you," he says.

"Thank you," I tell him – words far too inadequate to express the gratitude I feel. I smile and head out on a 7-mile walk, 2,385 feet up.

Because of my foot concern, I made a reservation to stop for the day in the small hamlet La Faba, only 5 miles away, rather than travel all the way to O'Cebreio. I arrive at my hostel sweating profusely from the grueling climb and the humidity in the forested trail. It was a hard climb, but oh so beautiful. Most of it was tree-lined. My heels had stayed quiet, but my thighs were screaming. I notice that when I'm going uphill and it suddenly gets steeper, my eyes don't perceive it, but the front of my thighs let me know — instantly.

I also notice that my clothes are starting to hang on me. When I passed by a window in the village, I saw my reflection. My shorts and tank top hang loose. It reminds me of exercise guru Richard Simmons. NOT a look I'm going for!

Tonight's hostel is next to the Iglesia San Andre (San Andres Church), operated by a German confraternity. The old stone building houses 66 beds, about half of them are in use today. In the afternoon I meet Allessio again, the young priest who I had roomed with a few weeks earlier. It's a joy to see a familiar face. He lights up when he sees me, too.

In the afternoon I watch a group of young people from Italy singing and laughing and sharing. Several are sitting on the edge of a fountain, cooling their feet in the water. I envy them. They're walking the Camino as part of a study program led by two Jesuit priests. I long for a sense of community and to have others to talk and share this experience with. Most of them eventually scatter to nap or do laundry and take care of business, but four remain in the courtyard, with guitar, singing. They speak very little English; I speak no Italian. Still, I approach and listen a while, then gain the courage to ask to borrow the guitar. I sing a few songs myself, songs I have written. They're impressed and appreciate I would share them.

Just that quickly, I'm connected, in communion and no longer alone. It strikes me how simple it is to move from being an outsider to being a part. Simple, but maybe not easy. It risks vulnerability and a willingness to venture out without knowing if I'll be accepted or not. I ventured. I was accepted. My heart is warmed.

In the evening I spend some time alone with the Lord. We talk about what I need to let go of to learn to love myself. To learn to really receive and love myself. I'm aware of attitudes and fears that work against me, so I mentally set them on an altar to burn, just like Much Afraid does in *Hinds' Feet on High Places*. It's not easy. It's a sacrifice to not think into and hold on to these feelings and beliefs. A sacrifice.

Day 27: August 4
La Faba to Hospital, 9 miles

The German host wakes us up bright and early. When I had checked in yesterday, he explained that in the morning he would wake us up with music at 6:00. "Oh good," I thought, remembering my first morning on Camino -- in Roncesvalles. A low light came on in the room and slowly grew brighter. At the same time, Gregorian chant music played softly and gradually grew louder until it was at a natural volume, and we were all awake. What a wonderful way to start the day! That had not happened since then.

126

However, now is not quite the same. Sharply at 6:00 a.m., the host flips a switch. Light abruptly shatters the calm of the darkness. It's offensive. Then he begins to move about the dorm, with an old boom box on his shoulder, playing music. Not the gentle Gregorian chant I was looking forward

Up early and ready to go

to . . . he's blaring *cumbia* dance music! Maybe that's strategic. It does make me move faster than usual. I'm up and dressed, filled with coffee and bread and on the trail by sunrise. One of the few times I've been out so early!

Throughout the day I continue to burn on the altar those attitudes that don't serve me; that aren't me. It's quite an emotional workout. Just as the remaining two miles straight up to O'Cebreiro is quite a physical workout. It's hard; I'm sweating heavily, but with a confidence that I will reach my goal.

Reaching the top, I stop for a brief rest, thankful that I made the climb so well. It's actually an enjoyable pain. I feel proud. I take a moment to sit in the 9th century *Iglesia de*

Santa Maria Real. The church marks the final resting place of Don Elias Valina Sampedro, the parish priest who is responsible for much of the restoration of the Camino. It was his idea to mark the route with the yellow arrows. I'm thankful that those arrows have guided me and thousands of others faithfully over many years.

The Pilgrim's Prayer written on the church wall tugs at my heart. Created by Franciscanos de Santiago, it reads in part:

> *Although I may have traveled all the roads,*
> *Crossed mountains and valleys from East to West.*
> *If I have not discovered the freedom to be myself,*
> *I have arrived nowhere. . . .*
>
> *If from today I do not continue walking on your path,*
> *Searching and living according to what I have   learned,*
> *If from today I do not see in every person, friend or foe*
> *A companion on the Camino; . . .*
>
> *I have arrived nowhere.*

Yes, I think. *What lessons from the Camino will stay with me? What will I take home? Will my life be different?* We'll see.

I had intended to stay in this town, but I feel so good, I decide to keep walking. The path is lovely. When I stop for a break I read a text from my friend Kathleen Horstmeyer. She's my contact person on this trip. I text her each day so that someone knows that I'm well and there's no need to worry. Today Kathleen writes that she had lunch with a small group of women yesterday. They had asked about me and commented that I'm amazing – a 65-year-old woman traveling the Camino alone.

"Oh, not really," I think to myself.

"Yes, really," is what I hear reverberate inside me. "You are an amazing woman. Stop acting like you're not. Own it."

I take a deep breath, pulling in the oxygen-rich air generated by the trees towering over me. I humble myself and accept the statement. I say it aloud to try it on: "I am an amazing woman."

I feel embarrassed, so I say it again, "I am an amazing woman."

Slowly the truth of such a bold statement begins to take root inside. As I say it again, I laugh. It's not the kind of laughter that comes because of embarrassment, but an honest laugh. It's fueled by a knowing that the statement rings true. I begin to believe it, to own it. I am amazing. I am a strong woman. A sexy woman. A loveable, desirable woman. That's me.

I put my backpack on and continue my journey uphill. I'm sweating heavily. Thankfully there's a cool breeze passing over the tree-lined path and across my body. It refreshes me, and I keep going all the way to Hospital. That's the name of a town, not a building. The community formed as a hospital to care for sojourning pilgrims many years ago. Now it is simply a small town. The end of today's route went up and down and up and down. My body is sore. It almost feels like I'm starting the Camino all over again. It's still challenging, but I have more confidence now. I have some newfound strength.

At the hostel I'm bored. There's nothing to do, nothing to see. Quite a few groups of 2 – 3 pilgrims are at the hostel, but they all keep to themselves. So I take a walk down the main road, stopping to watch a young man herd cattle through the street. More so, I watch his dog keep the cattle in

A working dog herds cattle through Main Street

line. When a cow would begin to separate from the small herd, the dog would quickly come alongside him and he would step back into line.

Then a woman stops me for a chat, a welcomed chat. When I share that I'm traveling alone on the Camino, she becomes very excited. She commends me for walking to Santiago, for making such a pilgrimage. The smile on her aged face opens wider with pride when she learns my age. I'll turn 65 tomorrow. I see my hopes and dreams reflected in her, and hers in me.

Yes, I think, *I am an amazing woman and so is she.*

Day 28: August 5
Hospital to Morgade, 8 miles (plus bus)

Happy birthday to me, I think to myself as I open my eyes. My 65th birthday. I'm experiencing it while on the walk of a lifetime. *Ah yes, I am an amazing woman*, I muse happily to myself.

When I left Albergue El Paso, I had calculated that I should plan eight days to travel from Sarria to Santiago. Many make it in half that, but I'm limited in how much I can cover in a day, so I planned on eight . . . just in case. The determining factor is that I have a bus ticket paid for from Santiago to Lisbon, Portugal. I plan to spend three days in Portugal and then catch my flight back home. That means I need to take the 7:40 a.m. bus from Hospital to Sarria today. I'm sad to by-pass another section, but it's for the best.

Sarria is an important city on the Camino. Of ancient Celtic origins, it became an important pilgrim stopping point in the 6th century. In present day, to receive the *Compostela* -- the certificate verifying you have indeed traveled the Camino -- pilgrims must have walked the last 100 kms (62.14 miles) or cycled the last 200 kms and have collected two stamps per day on their pilgrim credential. That means these last sixty miles of the road can become quite crowded. Many sojourners begin their walk in Sarria. Some get to Santiago and receive a Compostela after walking only 4-6 days.

I had read John Brierley's caution in his book, *A Pilgrim's Guide to the Camino de Santiago, Camino Frances*. He warned that pilgrims who have traveled long distances (such as me) need to be prepared for the sudden influx of new, energetic, and sometimes loud hikers.

> "Beware of signs of irritation at the intrusion of new pilgrims on 'my' camino. . . . None of us can know the inner motivation or outer circumstances of another. A loving pilgrim welcomes all they meet along the path with an open mind and open heart... without judgement of any kind."

I come to understand exactly what he meant.

Meanwhile, back to me. I easily get to Sarria by bus. Fortunately, another pilgrim, Ana from Poland, does the same. We walk together from the bus station, looking for the Camino markers to point us to the trail. We take a few wrong turns before finally finding our way. Once clearly on the marked path, we have breakfast together and then part as she moves quickly down the road.

The morning is such a beautiful time. There's lots of shade from the trees lining the road. There's a light breeze. I feel quite happy, quite blessed and pleased to be doing this. I sing and smile, thankful to be where I am. I set my attention on what I have – not on what I miss or don't have. I appreciate this wonderful way to spend my birthday.

I recall the woman I spoke with yesterday, the local who encouraged me on my journey. *I would like to have more encounters like that. I'd like to talk with more of the locals,* I think to myself. Almost instantly I happen upon a toothless old man, probably 80 or 90 years old, sitting on a bench in the shade of an old shack.

"*Mujer*! (woman)" he calls out. "Are you going to Santiago?" he asks in Spanish.

"Yes, I'm headed to Santiago" I answer him in Spanish. He giggles and asks me to sit with him, scooting over to make room.

I accept his invitation. I take a seat, but not beside him. I set my backpack on the ground and mount myself on the rock beside his bench. Our conversation is him repeatedly telling me how pretty I am. Now I appreciate that, I really do, but it's not quite the interaction I'm looking for. He smiles and holds his hand out to give me a walnut. I smile and accept it. He continues to flatter me as his body shifts, moving closer. We exchange a little small talk. He's a nice distraction and the shade is a welcome reprieve from the sun which is now beating harshly on the dirt path.

Still, I must continue on. I stand and put on my backpack to leave, despite him begging me not to. I tell him that I must go.

"Pray for me in Santiago," he says.

"What's your name?" I ask.

"Ignacio."

"Okay, Ignacio. I'll pray for you when I get to Santiago," I promise him. (And I did keep my promise.)

Ignacio gives me another nut, and then reaches his hand out to me. I shake it, put his nuts in my pocket – walnuts, just to be clear – and head down the road smiling as I listen to Ignacio giggle behind me.

I arrive in Morgade at 2:30 pm. and check in to my room. It's on the second floor, five twin beds side by side and windows on each end of the room. I'm thrilled! I won't be hot and sweaty tonight!

I return downstairs and order a salad with tuna. It's a lot of food, enough to hold me the rest of the day. I strike up a conversation with Gerde, a lovely woman from Austria. I proudly let her know that it's my birthday and I'm 65. Early evening she finds me and asks if she can treat me to a sangria for my birthday. Of course! It's a lovely and welcomed gesture. We sit and drink together and enjoy a very nice chat.

Tonight as I lay in bed I'm in awe of what I've done. Last year I had it in my heart to celebrate my 65th birthday on the Camino. Mission accomplished. It's such a good feeling to have achieved what I set out to do. There are so many times when I haven't followed through on one dream or another. This is a new beginning. This is a very good start for my 65th year.

Yet a far greater gift to myself is to accept that I am amazing. I am a special, beautiful woman with gifts and talents to bring to this world. And I'm not alone. I suspect every woman is amazing and it becomes apparent as she reaches inside and unlatches the door that holds her true self, hidden away and filling the role that others have cast her in. As she emerges, all will see and she will know, that she is an amazing woman. She will be able to laugh and embrace it.

An amazing woman

CHAPTER 9

Tears tumble and fall
For the hardships, the pain,
For the beauty, the glory,
The living, the vibrant, eternal
Joy of life.

Day 29: August 6
Morgade – Gonzar, 12 miles

Morning brings a cool stroll through country lands, green and lush. I'm really enjoying it. Feeling content. Reflecting a lot on my life and how good it is.

Wild flowers catch my attention and remind me of a passage in *Hinds' Feet*:

> ". . . the little wild flowers have a wonderful
> lesson to teach. They offer themselves so
> sweetly and confidently and willingly, even if it
> seems that there is no one to appreciate them.
> Just as though they sang a joyous little song to
> themselves, that it is so happy to love, even
> though one is not loved in return."

The Good Shepherd goes on to tell Much Afraid that some of our greatest victories are like the wild flowers, those which no one knows about. *This is a good lesson*, I think to myself. *A deep one.*

Flowers in boots, a tribute to passing pilgrims

By the time I finish today's walk my legs and hips are really feeling it. Twelve miles is a long ways for me. I check in, and grab a lower bunk by the door. This is a huge dorm – 34 beds divided into two rooms separated by two bathrooms. People are coming and going throughout the afternoon as I lay on my bed. It's hard to believe I can walk this many days (29), these many miles (183) and still be feeling pain as if it's something new!

At the same time, despite the pain, I feel such joy and lightness. I really enjoyed myself today. Maybe I've turned a corner on this pilgrimage.

The afternoon is pretty uneventful and a little boring. Despite so many people being here, I don't connect with anyone. It's raining, so I don't want to go outside. Instead, I take a long nap and do some reading.

Dinner is equally uneventful. I've mostly been eating the pilgrim menu along the way, but I'm getting tired of them. They're traditionally an appetizer such as salad, a main course always accompanied by potatoes, and a dessert. I think I'd be happy with just the salad, or something light. I notice that I'm not eating as much as I used to, and I'm losing weight. That's all good!

I'm in bed by 8:30 and slowly drift off to sleep.

Day 30: August 7
Gonzar – Portos, 7.5 miles

Everyone in the bunkhouse was up and out before 6:00 a.m. It's a funny feeling to be the only one left, but I am. I finally get up and am on the road myself by 6:45. However, after walking ten minutes, I conclude that there still isn't enough light for me to proceed confidently. It's too dark and I don't have a headlight like those who leave before sunrise. I can easily miss a yellow arrow and wind up lost in the middle of some field.

I sit on a bench in front of an old building and wait, enjoying the silence and the coolness of the morning. By 7:10 the sun is making his way up – at least sending rays over the hill enough to light my path. I move on. In the mist. In cool air. What a lovely time of day to be on the Camino!

After my second coffee stop it begins to rain. No problem. I have my poncho – a new thick one I bought in Sarria when I heard the reports about how rainy it would be traveling the remainder of the way. What is a problem, however, is that it rains just a little. I put on the poncho. I get hot under it and take it off when the rain stops. Then it starts to rain again and I put it back on. Off and on, off and on, off and on . . .

I stop for lunch at *Paso de Formiga* (Steps of the Ants). The owner shares that it is named after how pilgrims look when walking single file down the hill. It's only 12 noon and I would like to go further, but people are commenting that beds in Palas de Rei, where I want to go, are all booked.

I can't get service on my cell phone to make a reservation for a bed and I don't want to risk having to by-pass it and walk further. This is one of the downsides of so many new pilgrims joining in Sarria. There is greater likelihood that hostels will be full and a bed hard to find.

I've noticed that the road is becoming crowded now. I miss the solitude. I used to have up to three hours or so without seeing another soul. I really enjoyed that private time in nature. It was a wonderful gift. Now I'm getting as little as a half hour before others pass me by, entering my space, disrupting my *quietude*. That wouldn't be so bad, but sometimes they're talking on cell phones or being loud. I notice that often it's one person talking nonstop while the companions are reduced to just listening, probably as tired of hearing the droning voice as I am. Some are in large groups, laughing like they're at a party, or hurrying like they're in a race. I now understand why the guidebook warned us *veteran* pilgrims to not become resentful of the newbies on the road. I try, but I'm not very successful. Sometimes I give them a scowling look. Sometimes I take a seat on some stone or log to let them get far enough ahead of me to not have to listen to their noise.

Given the rain and potential lack of beds ahead, I check into Paso de Formiga hostel. I have a pleasant surprise of having two women from the United States as bunk mates. Nancy, from New York, is a librarian. We have a lot to talk about since I, too, have worked most of my life in libraries. Later we're joined by Kim.

After dinner I drink wine with Kim and listen to her heartbreak of unrequited love. That can easily happen when you're in love with a priest. My heart goes out to her. I wish I could offer some sage advice. Hopefully just giving a listening ear with an occasional nod of the head helps. It does seem that the Camino brings us quickly into very personal and vulnerable space with people. Or maybe it's the wine. Probably both.

Maybe it's the wine that also increases the snoring. Kim shares that her co-travelers who have moved on ahead said that she snores and they don't like to room with her. I understand. I sometimes snore, too. So I share with her my new secret weapon against snoring. It's small gauze-like tapes you put over your mouth to keep it closed while sleeping so that you won't snore. I've been using them on the trip. I give her a couple and she puts one across her lips when we turn out the lights to sleep.

Day 31: August 8
Portos – O'Coto, 9.5 miles

Okay, so I now know that my secret weapon doesn't work for everyone. Sadly, I heard Kim snoring last night. I don't mind. I understand. But now I'm quite embarrassed.

Back in Santa Catalina I had shared about this great invention with the doctors. I gave them a few so that they could try them out along the way. I used one myself as I slept in the bunk between them, with their sons on the bunks above us.

Funny thing is, the next morning as they prepared to leave before daylight, I was half awake as one of the sons reached down from his top bunk to retrieve his pillow from the floor beside my head. I had this eerie feeling that he had thrown it at me in the night to try to stop my snores. *Couldn't be*, I thought. *Or could it?* Now the evidence is in. Just like Kim, I likely was snoring through the night. Snoring through the closed lips. Snoring through the taped mouth. Probably snoring all across Spain!

Snoring is a common complaint in the hostels. There seems to always be at least one snorer. The guidebooks recommend that pilgrims bring earplugs to shut out the nuisance. I'm embarrassed to realize I may be the perpetrator of such nuisance.

I get up and move out. Along the way there are now markers stating how many kilometers are left to reach Santiago. Every time I pass one I feel a pang of sadness. I don't want it to end!

I walk mostly through tree-covered lanes today. I love it. Even the rain which continues off and on is no bother. I have plenty of stretches of solitude. I don't know where all the other pilgrims went today, but I appreciate their absence!

I feel as though I've gotten to know nature a little better, that we've deepened our personal relationship. The wind talks to me. So do the trees. It's wonderful. When I'm really quiet I think I can hear them whisper my name and impart sage wisdom from the ages. Something real and beautiful has opened in me, something that I know would not have happened without this Camino experience. It is life-changing.

To top off this exhilarating day, I treat myself to a hotel room for tonight's rest. Nice bed, clean sheets, private bathroom with towels and soaps . . . and television! I listen to the music stations, Spanish contemporary music. And I listen to the rain outside my window. It's a heavy rain that lasts through the night while I'm warmly tucked in my comfy room at *Dos Alemans*.

I think about where I've come. I realize I'm not complaining any more. I'm not feeling so lonely. I don't have so much pain . . . or maybe I'm just used to it. In any case, I feel good.

I also reflect on *Hinds' Feet*, the journey I've made with Much Afraid. She has reached the summit, the High Places of Joy. She has reached her goal and the Good Shepherd gives her a new name. She no longer is Much Afraid, she is Grace and Glory. He tells her "that when Love flowers in your heart you shall be loved again." I finish the book and go to sleep.

Day 32: August 9
O'Coto – Castaneda, 9.5 miles

Rain? Why yes, it continues to rain on me off and on. Actually, it's raining on everyone, not just me! It's kind of fun because a year earlier, back in Indiana I was walking in the rain one day. I wanted a downpour. I wanted to enjoy it like I did when I was a little girl running barefoot in the puddles. It was a fair, solid rain but there was no downpour. I was disappointed and added to my bucket list that I want to walk in the rain and get soaked.

So here I am. Finally, I get my fill of good, steady rain. Cloaked in my poncho, it's not bad. I get wet, but not drenched, so I don't know if this counts as fulfilling a bucket list wish or not. Maybe I'll just leave it on the list until I experience it without the covering of a rain poncho.

It's an all-around enjoyable day.

By noon the sun has come out, leaving drops of rain glistening on plants and flowers. I walk even slower than usual to appreciate the vibrant colors alongside the road. My reward for slowing and taking note of nature's bounty is a most spectacular spider web nestled in the bushes. Its symmetry is perfect. It's so delicate, so intricately woven. I'm impressed with this work of art. Now I wish there people around me, to point it out to, to share it with.

Walking and laughing in the rain

Passing through a small hamlet, I pause and watch a woman striking a stick on the ground, commanding her cattle to move out of the barn and down the street. "*Anda*," she cries out in an elderly and nasal tone. "*Echale, Alabar, ya.*"

I join in with her, "*Echale. Anda,*" I call out. We share a smile and I move on down the road with her cows. I love these simple wondrous moments.

I stop for the night in Castañeda, a small town, small hostel, and really small bathroom/shower. I'm the first one to check in and soon am joined by Ashley, a teacher from Chicago. We have a nice visit and I think it's going to be a nice relaxing night. Then a man and woman check in and our relaxation ends. The woman is a bit of a drama queen, changing the room dynamics. And so it is on the Camino – you never know what you'll get.

Day 33: August 10
Castañedo to Salceda, 10.5 miles

I wake up early and the rain is pouring heavily. I move slowly to see if it will let up before I get out on the road. By the time I finish my coffee at 8:15, it's weakened to a light drizzle.

By early afternoon the sun has come out. The rain has stopped and I'm ready to rest my feet. I pass a food stand to the side of the road, in the middle of a field. I order lemon beer, and it instantly becomes my new favorite drink. In my early days in Belorado when I was with John and Vicki, John had recommended it. I didn't drink one then, but I told him I would try one another day. Today's the day.

I love this lemon beer. I've never cared much for beer, don't like the taste in general. But this is light and on the sweet side.

(Note: When I returned to the USA I looked around until I found a good one. It's Stiegl Radler Zitrone Lemon, from Austria.)

While stopped, I take off my shoes to rest my feet and I do a blister check. I had a blister my first week and none since. I've kept them away after that by religiously

Lemon beer – a refreshing treat

greasing my feet with Vaseline and changing socks two to

three times a day, like I'm doing on this break. I read that tip about Vaseline in several posts on Camino forums when planning my trip.

It sounds counter-intuitive. How can smothering your feet in greasy Vaseline stop blisters? I don't know, but it's working for me. I only started doing this after I got that first blister. I haven't gotten another one since.

This is really important because I promised Blessed and Lovely I would take care of them.

"What? Blessed? Lovely?"

Those are my feet - the left one is Blessed; the right one Lovely. I named them before leaving for this trip. I thanked them for taking such good care of me these sixty plus years and promised I would listen to and take care of them. And truly, because of this Camino, I have learned to listen to them . . . I've learned to listen better to all my body. We've developed a new improved relationship in which I don't just demand what I want and force it to perform; but rather, I consult my body about what it needs—what *we* need.

The morning sky has left a soft cloud cover for the afternoon. Lots of shade trees. Soft breeze. Intimate time with my Lord. I'm coming to a conclusion about a conversation we've been having for some time now: I don't want to be alone.

In the three years since David passed, I've been content to be single. My friends and activities have kept me busy. I had no intention to look for another relationship, but

I had already begun to reconsider that. I was realizing I do want to be with someone. Now, at this point on the Camino, I know that I don't want to be alone. I do desire to have someone special in my life. It's a scary thought, though. I'm hesitant to embrace it, and I ask the Lord for help and guidance.

CHAPTER 10

What? One more hill?

Day 34: August 11
Salceda – Lavacolla, 13 miles

Today is a long walk. I haven't covered this many miles in one day since my trek through Pamplona my first week. What a time that was! What a very hard day that was! I'm stronger now. Also, it's not as hot now.

This morning holds a beautiful, fragrant walk through a eucalyptus grove. It's a great way to near my journey's end. Huge, towering trees. Calming. Inspiring. I sit for a while and just look at them. Tall. Confident. Majestic. I inhale their healing scent and close my eyes. Content. At peace.

As I move on, I find a young couple who are also inspiring to me: Jorge and Melissa. I walk behind them for a ways and admire the obvious love they share. The tender way they hold hands. I long for that. I invade their intimacy by snapping a picture. I can't resist. Then I quicken my gait to catch up with them.

"*Buen camino,*" I call out. Then stepping beside them, I tell them they're beautiful to watch, and I confess that I took their picture.

A tender moment in the eucalyptus grove

They don't mind. They unfold their story for me. Melissa is from Peru. She had been praying about becoming a nun, asking for God to give her a sign. When she traveled to Spain with her family to visit relatives she received her answer. She met Jorge and knew the convent was not in her future. They fell in love and began corresponding. A short time later she moved to Spain. They've been married four years now. Lovely couple. Loving story.

I, of course, do my usual crying. I don't mean to cry, but as they speak my heart is melting. I blubber through my tears that my husband died, that's why I'm here. Without missing a beat Melissa begins telling me to trust God, and she talks nonstop for about fifteen minutes as we walk. I don't know what all she's saying, it's too much to take in. But it does give me time to regain composure and dry my eyes.

I thank them for sharing and tell them their relationship is a beautiful thing to witness. I wish them well on their journey. I continue mine while they stop to rest.

Continuing through the tall, towering trees with my heart still feeling tender, I sense the Lord telling me we need to tend to one more blister. It's time to puncture it and draw it out.

I'm immediately transported back to an experience I had when David was very ill, a time when he was close to death. There were nights I hovered over his bed just to make sure he was still breathing. He could have simply drifted off at any time.

I felt I didn't want to live if he died. I had thought long and hard about it. I planned how I could end my own life once David passed on. Then it occurred to me that maybe he was tired of suffering and was ready to go now. I mustered up the courage one day to tell David what I had been thinking. I offered that if he wanted to go on to be with the Lord now, I'd like to cook us both up a little poison and end our lives now. We could both go. It was a simple picture in my mind . . . leave-taking. Just like every time we ever went to a party. We talked with friends, danced, ate, and laughed. Eventually one of us would look at the other and say, "Are you ready to go?" Then we'd make the rounds and say good-night to everyone. Just that easy.

That's the scene that was in my mind.

"Are you ready to go?"

When I suggested it to David he told me that he wasn't ready to go. With that statement, the thought immediately left my mind and I put all my strength back into living. It was another year before David did pass. By then I was no longer feeling the desire to die with him. I knew I needed to continue living.

Those feelings and that thought had not troubled me since then. But now the Lord is telling me that a seed of it is still deep in me, unpurged.

"It's time to get rid of the thought for good," I hear the Lord say. I sit on a log on the side of the path. As I cry a cleansing gush of tears, I let the feeling of wanting to die rise within me again, and then I let it go. I stand up, cleansed. I know I'm free of it forever. Life is precious and I'm determined more than ever that I will live it fully.

Later I check into my hotel room – yes, another special treat. It's my last night before I reach Santiago de Compostela. I take a long restful nap, tired after the 13-mile walk and drained from the emotional stirrings.

It's time for dinner in the hotel dining room and I had just plugged in my cell phone to charge. I decide to go to dinner without it. After all, part of what I'm learning on this journey is to be present, in the now. Along with that comes not being dependent on a cell phone for distraction.

The restaurant is full. Families and friends are engaged in conversation at every table while I sit alone at my big round table which seats four . . . with no cell phone. Nothing to make me look like I'm busy. Nothing to focus on, to keep me from having to see others in the room, or to notice them looking at me. I feel like this is a final exam – the ultimate test of being comfortable with myself, just me, without anything else or anyone else to lean on. It feels so awkward. I'm very uncomfortable. But I do it.

Looking back, I think this was my first step in learning not to be so dependent on my cell phone for comfort and companionship. I was beginning to let it go and just live in the present . . . an important lesson I continue to work on even now.

I look around the room and notice the other people. Sadly, what garners most of my attention is a man scolding a woman at the table in front of me. Her back is to me so I can't see her face, but his looks fierce and angry. He's big and round. He emotionally towers over her. He raises his voice, hits the table with the palm of his hand, stares her down. Sadly, it reminds me of scenes when I've sat in silence and let someone degrade me like that. I want to step over and tell her she should leave; that she deserves better. Regretfully, I don't.

Back home, that image has stayed with me. I'm aware of changes within myself since then. I suspect that if I were to see such a display again, I just might have the courage to say something to the woman. Maybe. I do know I wouldn't just sit and take it if I were in her place. That's for sure.

Day 35: August 12
Lavacolla – Santiago, 8 miles

My last day. Say it isn't so!

I'm on the road by 8:00 a.m. – the crowded road. Oh how I miss my quiet time! I'm especially resentful when one man *teases* me as he passes by, saying that it will take me two days to get to Santiago at the rate I'm walking. "*Andalé!* Step it up!" he says as he laughs, moving swiftly down the road surrounded by his children.

My response: "You don't know me! You know nothing about what I've done, where I've come from. I began this journey almost 500 miles ago; you probably just jumped on the road a couple of days ago. You don't know what I've been through to get here. You don't know how badly my feet hurt. You have no right to say anything to me about the pace I'm walking. This is my Camino, not yours."

Yes, that's my response . . . in my head. That's what I wish I would have said to him aloud. It's taken me a half hour to think of that comeback and he's long gone now, out of sight. Instead, I had only given him a gnarly look and kept my mouth shut.

I continue to think of that as I walk on down the road. Who does know another person's journey? Who really knows what someone else has been through, what challenges, fears, experiences? It's easy to jump in and comment on what we see, but we see only an exterior. We don't see the inside of a person. That only comes when we've developed a relationship of trust that lets someone in to share with us, and us with them. I hope that this will be seared in my memory as a lesson to not judge. I don't know another person's *camino*.

Breaking that thought, another pilgrim walks past, commenting that we have only one more hill to climb.

"What? One more hill?" I say in dismay. "I thought these final miles were a straight shot into the city."

They aren't. We laugh and keep moving. We have to ascend *Monte de Gozo* (Mountain of Joy), one last hill before Santiago. From here pilgrims get their first glimpse of the mighty spires of the cathedral. It is said that in medieval times the pilgrims would fall to their knees, shouting and singing with joy at the sight of the cathedral. Destination is in sight!

When I get to the top of the hill, I don't fall to my knees. I don't sing. From the hilltop I do, however, appreciate the sight of the cathedral in the distance . . . a place that I will reach soon, sadly. I don't want the pilgrimage to end. I want to keep going, unsure of what life will be like when I return home, afraid maybe I haven't gotten everything I need from the Camino.

 I reach the city in early afternoon, stopping to take a selfie in front of the sign: Santiago. *I made it*, I think to myself. *I'm here.*

I look forward to getting to the cathedral. I wonder what it will feel like to arrive. Will I cry? Will I feel an overwhelming joy? A good friend had emailed me this week and encouraged me to prepare my heart and soul for entering Santiago, to milk every last spiritual moment out of the journey that I can. *Yes*, I think. *Let me stay present and in the spirit of a pilgrim.*

I walk on the sidewalk, passing office buildings, banks, restaurants, and every sort of site you would expect to see in a city. Traffic is passing swiftly by, paying no mind to me or the other occasional pilgrim here and there. Noise is constant. When I lose the markings on the sidewalk, I resort to my iPhone GPS to lead me toward the cathedral. It's really hot. I'm sweating. I'm starting to realize that it is no short distance from the welcoming city sign to the old section in its center. I cross street after street.

I arrive at a cathedral off to the side of a busy street. I'm surprised at how small it is and that there aren't a lot of people in the plaza it surrounds. I stop an elderly woman walking across it and in Spanish ask her if this is the cathedral.

"Oh no," she says with a smile. "It's much further," and she points me on down the way.

I thank her and keep walking. I've picked up the yellow arrows on the sidewalks again, though they sometimes disappear. At one five-way intersection I see a group of pilgrims (believe me, you can always spot them) across the street, heading away from me. But the arrows show me crossing the street in the opposite direction. I feel frustrated, tired, and slightly confused. I follow the arrows, and wouldn't you know it, they lead me down a short ways, across the street and backtrack me to where those pilgrims had stood. Go figure.

I just want to finish now. I want it to be over. I'm no longer sad about this being the last day. As I walk I wonder if this design of ending the pilgrimage by traversing a busy city is a strategy to prepare one for re-entry into normal life. For me, all the *spiritual* and *holy* sense of the Camino has ended in these last two hours of a grueling walk on hard pavement and concrete, in the heat, dodging traffic and putting up with nonstop city sounds and sights, while trying to scope out the markers to find my way. It seems like it will never end.

Finally, I turn a corner and step onto Plaza de Obradoiro, the plaza facing the cathedral. It's a dramatic sight. I have to laugh at myself to have mistaken the small ordinary church I passed earlier as possibly being the cathedral. Not a chance! The Cathedral de Santiago is grand. It's majestic. Its plaza is filled with pilgrims and tourists. I enjoy seeing pilgrims laying in the square, or sitting with their backs against backpacks for support as they admire the building and reflect on their journeys. I set down my pack and take a seat among them.

I'm impressed, but too tired to react. I don't even cry. I feel numb, too tired to put any meaning into what just happened. I arrived. Mission accomplished.

Cathedral de Santiago de Compostela

I walk several blocks more to find the hotel where I have a reservation. As I lay on my bed, I start to process the day. Perhaps this is how it should be. Perhaps it's a well thought out plan to help move us along back into our lives. In the end, I see that re-entry has taken care of itself. I'm quickly back into my normal life.

I truly know that's the case once I get up from my nap and go shopping. I buy a new dress. Can you imagine how tired I am of wearing the same two shorts, one pant and three tops over 35 days? I understand that in the early days the pilgrims would burn their clothes when they reached their destination. I would love to do that, but then what ...? No, that's not an option for me, but a new dress is very much appreciated.

I make my way back across the plaza and find the Pilgrim's Office where I will present my Pilgrim's passport and get my compostela, the certificate which verifies I successfully completed my hike on the Camino de Santiago. I'm stopped at the door and told they can't take any more pilgrims in today. There is already a waiting line that will take them to closing time to process. I should return in the morning. Thankfully, I have tomorrow free to explore the city. I'll take a bus out the day after.

Day 36: August 13
The Compostela

Rested and refreshed, I'm up early to get my number to line up at the Pilgrim's Office. An hour later, I feel a surge of joy and pride as I stand before the officer at the counter. I

161

watch him examine my pilgrim's passport filled with the stamps which document my journey.

I feel accomplishment as he prints my name on the certificate. I walked 253. Not bad for a 65-year old woman who has lived a mostly sedentary life. I've accomplished what I set in my heart to do.

The rest of the day I walk about, shopping for a few souvenirs – nothing big since I'm still using only my backpack. I take a tour of the cathedral and its surroundings. Unfortunately for me, the cathedral is undergoing restoration and it's not open to host the traditional Pilgrim's Mass. I would have enjoyed that, but in the end, I'm content with just being here, witnessing this UNESCO heritage site. And besides, my feet do still hurt quite a bit.

Before returning to my hotel room I make one final purchase. Make-up. I haven't used make-up for over a month. I step into a store I'm not familiar with. Kiko. The salesgirl does my make-up for me and I buy the basics. I step out the door feeling normal again. Feeling amazing.

Day 37: August 14
One Last Thing

I began my pilgrimage with Amy Kim, the young woman I met the night we arrived in St. Jean Pied de Port – wet and tired. We traveled together to Roncesvalles, then were separated by different walking speeds the next day. I saw her again two and a half weeks later when we ended up at the same hostel in Rabanal. I don't think it was any accident. She showed up just in time to accompany me to *Cruz de Ferro*, where I said my final goodbye to David. It was good to have a friend to walk that road with me. As is the way of the Camino, we got separated again after that until Vega de Valcarce where she spent an extra day and I spent a couple of extra days.

Amy reached Santiago a few days ahead of me and traveled on to Finesterre on the coast. It's another three or four days of walking, or a half day bus ride, and it's popular among pilgrims to continue to the sea, until they can go no further. Before the days of Columbus, it was thought that this coast literally was the "end of the world," thus the name. Amy returned to Santiago to take a bus to Porto, Portugal on August 14, the same day I have a bus ticket to Lisbon, Portugal. Through email contact, we're happy to learn that our buses depart within a half hour of each other. It's only fitting, and most wondrous, that on my last day in Spain I connect with Amy once again.

We meet at the bus station for a final swapping of stories and hugs and good wishes, and a final *buen camino* as she boards her bus. Mine leaves a half hour later. It takes me to Lisbon where I'll explore the sights and the culture for three days before taking a flight home to the USA.

Amy and Cathay final rendezvous, Santiago bus station

AFTERWARD

"Sometimes you will never know the value of something
until it becomes a memory."
--Dr. Seuss

It has been a year since I boarded an airplane to Europe, since I made a pilgrimage to Santiago de Compostela. In the first months after returning home I was still wondering what the walk had been about, wondering if I had gotten everything from it that I was meant to get. It took just over a month to walk the Camino, but it has taken many more months for its impact to travel from my soul to my mind. Its messages are still unraveling, still taking on new depth.

After a year my heels have finally calmed down. I've realized it was a combination of Achilles tendonitis and bursitis that I developed. I rested my feet (Blessed and Lovely) for some time and now they do not hurt *as much* when I walk – and I still try to walk at least a mile or two every day. I love to walk, especially in nature. I love to walk through parks, trails and forested areas as much as possible. It renews my spirit. It makes me feel grateful.

I like the physical activity of walking, but more than that, I've come to believe that it is the best way to really get to know a place – to walk it. To step on its soil. To pass through it slowly enough to listen, to hear the beating of its life force and get a glimpse of its character. I was driving on the highway through Montana one day and had the most incredible urge to leave my car and walk through the golden fields on the hills lining the highway. Up and down and up and down. Sadly, that is not practical.

It has also taken just over a year to write this book, and it is in writing this book that I am beginning to better understand the purpose of my Camino and its gifts to me.

The first thing I noticed immediately after I finished, is that I laugh more easily and bigger than I ever have in my life. I first saw it in a picture taken in Lisbon, Portugal after the Camino. My head is thrown back in laughter. Over what? I don't know. I don't remember, but surely the photographer and I were sharing some funny comment. I looked at my face in that photograph and realized I had never experienced such free expression before. Looking back through the rest of my pictures, I see a few more examples of that same delightful abandon on my face.

166

I can't pinpoint the details of it, but I know that somehow, somewhere, some small internal latch had released its hold, freeing me of some inhibition. I am more at ease, more accepting of myself, more gentle with myself.

Is that the result of absolution? I'm reminded of my first day in Roncesvalles, in the church where I heard the word *absolution* whispered in my spirit. "I'm here for me to absolve myself of judgment I hold against me. I'm here to forgive myself; to come to know and love myself and to release myself of guilt."

Weeks later fellow pilgrim Patrick had said to me, "You're here [on the Camino] to learn to fall in love with yourself again." Have I? Have I forgiven myself? Fallen in love with myself? I think so. I think this freedom to express myself in laughter is the result of absolution. It is evidence that I love me, that I no longer feel a need to hide myself. I am vulnerable, and that's okay. It is good.

I think about other treasures, other gifts the Camino gave me. Early on I had written to friends back home that "I am learning to trust God in a new way. I'm learning that I am not in control," I wrote. "*The Camino* is in control. I just follow it up and down, on smooth ground, hard ground, over loose rock and endless dirt surfaces with no end in sight. I just keep walking."

What I've come to know is that I am in control. I make my decisions about my life, just as I decided to walk the Camino, just like I decided multiple times not to quit and go hang out at a luxury hotel instead. What I gave up control over was having to know every step in advance. I gave up control of the need to know what would happen; the need to have the answers. I learned to let go of that control and trust God in it. That's a very liberating experience, especially when you consider I can't control those things anyway! I can, however, choose to live in this moment and control what I do with it, how I create it and how I react to it.

That was another gift – becoming mindful, being present. It didn't come easily. My mind continually wanted to look ahead and imagine what might happen next or when I get home, or to look back and revisit yesterday's walk. I persistently kept drawing it back to the present moment. Even sitting alone in the wonder of nature, I repeatedly had to wrestle my mind into stillness. I still have to, but it is easier now. I've experienced it enough to appreciate the calm and centering of self that being still brings.

I recall my last night on the Camino, sitting in a restaurant without my cell phone. It felt like a *final exam* in learning to be present, and to be comfortable with myself, just myself. It puzzled me for some time even after I left the Camino. What was that about? I was reminded of it when I read *The 5 AM Club, Own Your Morning, Elevate Your Life* by Robin Sharma. I connected with his description of how dependent we are on our cell phones and technology . . . how that we look for distraction. I could totally relate. He wrote that most people can't stand themselves, so they can never be alone.

"They need to constantly be with other people
to escape their feelings of self-hatred over all

their wasted potential, missing the wonders and wisdom that solitude and quiet bring."

Ah, that's it, I realized. That *final exam* was another experience in learning to love myself, to be content with just myself. I can't say I aced that exam, but I think I got at least a passing score. It's an area in which I'm still learning and still growing.

When I was preparing to walk the Camino, I knew it was something I needed to do alone. It was a pilgrimage I needed to make without distractions, without relying on others to keep me company. It was an opportunity to go inward, just me and my Lord. It was important for me at that time in my life.

Traveling solo helped me to realize that I didn't want to live the rest of my life, my next thirty years, alone. I didn't know what those next thirty years would bring, but I wanted to share them with someone. I had been blessed in my marriage with David and it was hard to imagine having such a relationship with anyone else. Yet that is just what I wanted. I decided to be open to it.

Four months after returning home I met Ray Corder and have been with him ever since. I was surprised at how quickly he entered my life, how comfortably we fell into step with each other, and how easily our love blossomed. The truth is I was preparing for this relationship for a very long time. I was ready when he came along. And in case you're wondering . . . yes, we often hold hands when we walk. When we do, I think of the young couple I photographed holding hands.

I'm more settled, more centered these days. I have a better relationship with my body and know better how to listen to it. I have resolve in my soul to live every day fully with gratitude and thanksgiving. Life is precious, and it is beautiful.

Above all, I have absolved myself of all judgement I held against me. I have learned to love myself. I can say that through struggles and pain, I kept walking . . . and my heart did catch up.

I know more about me than I did a year ago. I know...

I can do anything.
I am unstoppable.
I am an amazing woman.